3 easy steps to the

JOB YOU WANT

3 easy steps to the

JOB YOU WANT

MALCOLM HORNBY

Prentice Hall

an imprint of **Pearson Education**

London • New York • San Francisco • Toronto • Sydney • Tokyo • Singapore • Hong Kong
Cape Town • Madrid • Paris • Milan • Munich • Amsterdam

PEARSON EDUCATION LIMITED

Head Office:
Edinburgh Gate
Harlow CM20 2JE
Tel: +44 (0)1279 623623
Fax: +44 (0)1279 431059

London Office:
128 Long Acre
London WC2E 9AN
Tel: +44 (0)207 447 2000
Fax: +44(0)207 240 5771

Website www.business-minds.com

First published as *I Can Do That!* 1993
Second edition 1994
Third edition published as *36 Steps to the Job You Want* 1998
This edition first published in Great Britain in 2000

© Pearson Education Limited 2000
The right of Malcolm Hornby to be identified as author of this work has been asserted by him
in accordance with the Copyright, Designs and Patents Act 1988.

ISBN 0 273 65245 1

British Library Cataloguing in Publication Data
A CIP catalogue record for this book can be obtained from the British Library

10 9 8 7 6 5 4

Designed by Claire Brodmann Book Designs, Burton-on-Trent
Typeset by Northern Phototypesetting Co Ltd, Bolton
Printed and bound in the United Kingdom by Biddles of Guildford Ltd

The Publishers' policy is to use paper manufactured from sustainable forests.

CONTENTS

Step 1   WHO AM I?

To help you put your jobsearch into the context of your whole life   1

Introduction to Step 1

ACTIVITIES

Step 2   WHERE AM I GOING?

ACTIVITIES

Step 3   HOW WILL I GET THERE?

ACTIVITIES

DEDICATION

3 easy steps to the job you want is dedicated to my Dad, Joe Hornby, who was made redundant in 1969, after 38 years as a miner.

It is also dedicated to you, the reader. I hope that what you gain from this workbook will help you to quickly find rewarding and meaningful work – like my father did.

Pass it on

Do you have a jobsearch anecdote which will be of benefit to others, or a novel way to tap into the unadvertised job market? If you have, write to me at the address below and we'll include it in the next edition.

Malcolm Hornby c/o Prentice Hall

128 Long Acre, London WC2E 9AN, UK

Alternatively e-mail me: Malcolm@TheJobSearchersSuperstore.com

ACKNOWLEDGEMENTS

The idea for this book was mine, but it would never have become a reality without the help, support and advice of a great number of people.

I am especially grateful to the 'real life' career planners and jobsearchers who have provided a 'reality check'. Knowing how useful the activities have been to them was the inspiration to start the book, and has sustained me through many long hours at my desk.

I am also grateful to the people below, whose advice as critical readers has helped me in the development of *3 easy steps to the job you want*. Their candid advice (if at times difficult to take!), based on their experience, has been invaluable. I am sure that, in turn, it will help you in your jobsearch. Thank you. (Job titles and organisations at time of writing.)

Gary Dickinson
Vice President, Human Resources, Bristol-Myers

John Lomax
Business Planning Manager, British Telecom

Roger Walker
Principal Consultant, Chamberlain Walker

Pat O'Brien
Principal Consultant, Patrick O'Brien & Associates

Christine Sanham
HRD Consultant, Christine Sanham

Carmel Capewell
CMC

Steve Dyke
Operations Manager, Courtaulds

Jan Denton
Manager, Opus, Devon and Cornwall Training & Enterprise Council

Jon Passmore
Chief Housing Officer
East Northamptonshire District Council

Robin Turner
National Sales Manager, Fisons Plc

Martin Scott
Programme Manager, G E Thorn

Nichola Balmer
Marketing Manager, Gent Ltd

Jim O'Mahoney
Operations Director, Grand Metropolitan

Ann Keenan
Training & Development Manager
Hitchingbrook Health Care

Robert Appleyard
Production Controller, Ilmor Engineering

Ian Burch
Director, IRD Services

Soleveig Bruce-Stupples
Human Resources Manager
Pharmacia Ltd

Elspeth May
Partner, KPMG Peat Marwick

Bob Dutton
Senior Assistant Education Officer/FE
Leicestershire County Council

Phil Laughton
Central Area Librarian
Leicestershire Libraries

Roland Powell
Manager, New Product Planning – Europe
Lilly International Corporation

Sue Walder
Premises & Facilities Manager
NEC Electronics (UK) Ltd

Margaret Gale-Smith
Corporate Training Manager
Northampton Borough Council

Linda Smith
MEC, The Open University

Brian O'Hara
Chairman, Penn Pax Products Limited

Tony Perryman
Personnel Director, Presto Stores Ltd

Pauline Kinns
Training Manager, RTCC Ltd

Sadie Green
Freelance Trainer, Sadie Green

Tracy Smeathers
Personnel Officer, Scott Bader Ltd

Rick Woodward
Management Development Manager
The Wellcome Foundation

Thank you also to Roy Davis of SHL, Bob Edenborough of ASE, Barbara Walsh, Regional Resettlement Advisor, RAF Brampton, Simon Parker at Monster.co.uk and Andrew Banks and Geoff Morgan of TMP Worldwide, all of whom have been kind enough to contribute to *3 easy steps to the job you want* and to Richard who did the illustrations.

Thank you to Rachael Stock at Pearson Education for her advice and guidance.

Final thanks go to Bernie, my wife, for her help and support throughout the project, and to Carla and Jan who reminded me of the benefits of taking a break occasionally, to 'stop and smell the roses'. (Carla's our German Shepherd dog and Jan, our Border Collie!)

Equal opportunity statement: I have made every effort to make the text of this book non-discriminatory. If I have failed in any part, please let me know, so that I can correct it for future editions

M.H.

'Would you tell me … which way I ought to go from here?' asked Alice.

'That depends a good deal on where you want to get to,' said the Cat.

Lewis Carroll

Why I wrote this book … why you need this book

I can give you a six word formula for success: 'Think things through – then follow through.'

Edward Rickenbacker

Welcome. This book will help you to take control of your life, plan your career and get the job you want.

WHY I WROTE THIS BOOK

This is the fourth version of this book, which I first self-published as *I Can Do That!* in 1993. Since then it has become one of the publisher's best sellers and has been translated into many languages. More important, though, it has helped thousands of people to find a new career direction, and to get a new job.

I was inspired to write the original version of *3 easy steps* when I first started working with groups of people who had been made redundant in 1990.

It is often a major 'life-event' such as redundancy, divorce or leaving university that triggers people into taking stock of what they want to get out of life. But it doesn't have to be. What's needed is the determination that you want the best out of life.

It sounds hackneyed, but 'life isn't a rehearsal'. It happens in 'real time'. I'm a firm believer that to get the best out of life, you need to take control of your own destiny.

My objective was to produce a 'self-managed' personal development programme in a book, which would help people to take stock of what they really want out of life. By using the exercises and techniques, you'll identify what makes you special, you'll set your own career and life goals and you'll learn about techniques which can help you to get the job you want.

WHY YOU NEED THIS BOOK

Prior to writing *3 easy steps* I was Head of Personnel in the UK for Bristol-Myers & Clairol and have taught human resource strategies at Masters level. In *3 easy steps* I've blown the whistle on many techniques that are used by personnel managers, so that you can use them in your jobsearch.

The book contains everything you'll need to draw up your career and life plan and the techniques to help you get the job you want: from personality profiling and career–life balance exercises, to practical tips on how to write a CV and letters of application, access the unadvertised job market, use positive body language, use the internet and how to make a presentation.

By owning this book you have also become a member of our worldwide internet community, dedicated to helping you to plan your career and find the right job. www.TheJobsearchersSuperstore.com will take you there. Why not pay us a visit?

YOU CAN CONTROL YOU DESTINY

For most of us, our working and personal lives are intertwined. Career planning is the process of formulating goals, for what we want to achieve in our working lives. This has an inevitable impact on our personal lives.

Without goals, your career (and your life) could be shaped by accident, fate or even by the decisions by other people. This may lead to dissatisfaction or frustration. By setting your own goals, you can take control of your own career development and your own life. The foundation of our career and life planning process is knowing who you are. Being able to identify your own strengths, skills and values is vital in setting realistic career goals. These will help you to make decisions about your career and about opportunities available to you.

By working through the activities in this book you will have a clearer idea of where you are now, where you are going and how you will get there.

SELF-ASSESSMENT

Step 1 is 'understanding myself'. This will help you to develop a more enlightened picture of who you are and what you want out of life.

We will then go on to identify how you can match your skills to jobs effectively through a greater personal understanding and an understanding of how to secure a new job.

Not all the sections in this workbook will be equally relevant to you. Your own career and life situation, age, position, values, etc., will determine the areas you need to explore in greatest depth.

People change. Your interests and goals may change over time. By completing this workbook, you are embarking on a process, through which you will be able to establish realistic career goals and an action plan to achieve them: not just where you want to go, but also what you have to do to get there. You will learn to manage your career so that you can make informed judgements about the job opportunities that become available to you in the future.

UP, SIDEWAYS, DOWN

A 'promotion' is one way of developing in your career. However, it isn't the only way, and as organisations become 'leaner' and reduce the number of levels, the opportunities are becoming fewer.

Enriching your present position can be another important form of career development. So is acquiring a new set of skills, or taking on a temporary developmental assignment. In some cases, your best decision may be to move laterally into another area, or perhaps even take a step downwards to acquire new skills and experience.

YOU ARE RESPONSIBLE FOR YOUR CAREER AND YOUR LIFE

The responsibility for managing your career is yours. Take the initiative.

Remember that your career is only one important strand in the fabric of your life. The decisions you make about your career can have an impact on other dimensions of your life – just as the decisions you make in your personal life can affect your career. The exercises in this workbook will help you develop a greater awareness of what you need to do to keep all the dimensions of your life in healthy balance.

KEEP AN OPEN MIND AND BE FLEXIBLE

People often have problems in making career plans and developing goals because they impose barriers on themselves. They say to themselves things like 'I could never achieve this', 'That opportunity is not available to me', 'This isn't feasible', etc.

Keep an open mind as you work through the activities in this book. As a general rule people impose more restrictions on themselves than are imposed on them by other people.

INVEST IN YOURSELF – YOU'RE WORTH IT

Don't be put off by the length of this workbook. It won't take long to complete.

Complete one or two activities at a time. You will get the best benefit if you complete the workbook in a continuous period of two to four weeks. You will find the process takes on a momentum of its own.

The benefits you obtain from this workbook will be in direct proportion to the effort you put into completing them. It may be tempting to read through the exercises and 'complete them in your head'. Do that as a starting point, but you will only really benefit by sitting down, pencil in hand!

To put what I've said in context: Most people spend more money on an annual holiday than they'll spend in the whole of their lives on self-development. Most people spend more time choosing a new car than they do planning what they want to do with the rest of their lives. Invest in yourself – you're worth it.

CONCENTRATE ON AREAS RELEVANT TO YOU

As already mentioned, not all sections of this workbook will be equally relevant to you.

CONSULT OTHERS

Career and life planning means integrating information about you – your interests, skills and potential. You will understand yourself better if you check your own perceptions against those of people who know you well – your friends, partner, colleagues, etc.

But before we begin, some ground rules.

- This workbook is about you.
- To get the best out of the exercise you need to be as open and honest with yourself as you can.
- At times I will suggest that you might want to discuss certain aspects confidentially with other people. This will give you the opportunity to 'test' some of your ideas. Remember, what you let other people know about you and what you decide to keep close is entirely in your control.
- You may wish to keep your workbook somewhere private.
- We are all unique and for that reason each person will derive different benefits from different exercises. The common threads will be improved self-awareness and a greater chance of securing the right job for you.
- It is not essential to complete every exercise.
- There is a job out there for you.

DOES IT WORK, WILL IT BE WORTHWHILE?

It gives me a tremendous buzz when I hear from people who have used the techniques in my book to land a job. Like Peter, for instance, a manager who had been unemployed for a year. Peter had applied for hundreds of jobs, without success. After using one technique from *3 easy steps*, he landed a job within a week. Or Heather, a school leaver, who followed the advice in *3 easy steps* and got the first job she applied for, as a trainee veterinary nurse. John had been unhappy in his job in management for over a decade, he was 'liberated' by redundancy and used the techniques from this book to take some easy steps into a job as a college lecturer.

Go for it!! And …
Good luck.

Malcolm Hornby

WHO AM I?

The word "WHO" and "AM I" are formed from densely packed job titles:

...utiveAcc...
...strator Advertising...
...aft Engineer Airline Pilot A...
...mal Technician Anthropologis...
...okseller Antique Dealer Archaeo...
...rchitect Archiver Art Dealer Astron...
...uctioneer Ballet Dancer Banker Barr...
Biochemist Botanist Bookseller Broad...
Broker Builder Careers Advisor Cart...
Cardiologist Chemical Engineer Chir...
Clerk Coastguard Community Worke...
...cretary Computer Engineer Conduct...
...igner Dentist Development Engin...
...tor Dispensing Optician Docto...
...rainer Draughtsman Driving...
...ist Economist Editor Educat...
...cal Engineer Electronic Engir...
...ainer Environmental He...h...
...nomist Estate Agent E...
...ort Agent Fabric Desig...
...rm Manager Fashion Ph...
...ilm Director Financial Ma...
...ish Farmer Flight Controller...
...nologist Footwear Manufacture...
...Office Executive Forensic Scientist...
...Forwarder Game Keeper Geneticist G...

...rographic Survey...
...ormation Scientist Insura...
...terior Designer International...
...vellery Designer Journalist Land...
...awyer Legal Accountant Librarian...
...ousekeeper Loss Adjuster Magazine...
...Management Accountant Marine Eng...
...Marketing Manager Media Planner M...
...hysicist Merchant Banker Metallurgi...
...Microbiologist Missionary Model Mu...
...Naval Architect Neurophysiologist N...
...ngineer Nurse Occupational Thera...
...ce Manager Optician Packagin...
...ter Patent Agent Personnel M...
...macist Physicist Pianist Poli...
...ter Probation Officer Psychia...
...ublic Administrator Publis...
...reational Manager R...
...ager School Inspector...
...erson Silversmith Socio...
...oker Surveyor Systems An...
...Textile Designer Theatre Ma...
...g Standards Officer Travel Agen...
...erwriter Veterinary Surgeon Wate...
...outh Worker Zoo Keeper Zoologist Z...

To help you put your jobsearch into the
context of your whole life

INTRODUCTION TO STEP 1

All things I thought I knew; but now confess the more I know I know, I know the less.

John Owen

ARE YOU A FROG OR A PIKE?

Frogs are remarkably adaptable creatures. Apparently, if exposed to near-freezing conditions, they have the ability to slow down their metabolism and to go into hibernation. If you then take one of these frogs and place it in cold water, it becomes more active and increases its metabolism. As the water temperature increases, so does the activity of the frog. The frog makes no attempt to escape from its surroundings ... even if the temperature of the water is increased to the point where it is boiled to death!

So while being adaptable, the frog fails to challenge what is happening around it. By being unprepared to move to a different environment, the frog pays the price of its life.

In a similar sort of way, if you take a pike and place it in a large aquarium and then add a few minnows, I am sure you will not be surprised to hear that the minnows are very quickly eaten by the pike.

If a glass partition is now placed in the aquarium with the pike in one half and more minnows in the other half, the pike will make attempt after attempt to eat the minnows, but only succeeds in hitting the glass! The pike finally learns that attacking the minnows is an impossible task.

If the glass partition is now removed and the minnows and pike are allowed to swim freely in the tank you might 'naturally' imagine that the pike would resume eating. Surprisingly, the pike fails to recognise that the environment has changed and does not eat the minnows. In fact the pike will starve to death!

HOW CAN I DEVELOP A RECIPE FOR SUCCESS?

A major step may be to challenge your paradigm:

A paradigm is a set of rules and regulations that describe boundaries and tell you what to do to be successful within those boundaries.

(definition by Joel A. Barker, *Discovering the Future*, ILI Press)

But, of course, frogs and pikes are very simple animals. Human beings are far more sophisticated and should be more open to change … would that it were the case! Most of us try to find solutions to our problems using our current paradigm of the situation. For example, doctors use their medical training to form a diagnosis. This works well until either we cannot solve a problem using our paradigm, or someone generates another totally different paradigm for solving the problem which we will not accept. For example, many doctors do not recognise 'fringe medicine' such as acupuncture because, in spite of any success, those approaches do not conform to their own training and beliefs.

In business, people are blinded by their current paradigms to new approaches, whether they are developed internally or by competitors. Swiss watch manufacturers dismissed the concept of the Quartz watch, the prototype of which was created in 1967 by the Swiss Watch Federation. Before World War II the Swiss had 90 per cent of the watch market, by the 1970s they had 60 per cent, but by 1980 they had only 22 per cent.

Similarly, 42 photographic companies rejected Chester Carlson's new photographic process in 1930 because it did not relate to their paradigm of photography. One company did have foresight – the Xerox Corporation.

Most of us can become better at generating new solutions if we:

- listen to others with a totally different view (they probably have a different paradigm)
- listen to our own intuition and have faith in our own absurd ideas rather than suppressing them.

If you cannot generate new solutions, keep your mind open to others' ways of doing thing and see if they are worth copying. IBM copied Apple's radical approach to enter the PC market; Wimpy copied McDonald's by becoming counter service rather than table service restaurants.

What have frogs and pikes got to do with career planning and jobsearching? Well, everything! Our working environments are changing faster than ever. The rate of change continues to accelerate. A couple of decades ago, no one had heard of HTML, Perl, C++ or Java. Now people who can speak these IT and website assembly languages can almost pick their salary! There is no 'one way' to plan your career or to find a new job; the keys to maximising your potential are flexibility, keeping an open mind and regarding change as an opportunity not a threat.

'Seeing is believing' – our beliefs and perceptions about what is right or possible often prevent us from exploring new solutions. Remember what happened to the frog and the pike!

(*Author's note*: The experiments quoted are 'classic' experiments which have been carried out in the past by behavioural scientists. Refs: The frog – *Shaping Your Organisation's Future, Frogs, Dragons, Bees and Turkey Tails*, J. William Pfeiffer *et al.*, Pfeiffer & Co San Diego; The pike – Eden Ryl, Ramic Productions Film, 'Grab Hold of Today'. I assure you that I have neither boiled frogs, nor starved pike to death – MH.)

ACTIVITY 1

Allow me to introduce myself

 Know thyself.   Chilo (BC 560)

3 easy steps to the job you want is about you. This five-minute activity will help you to think about your past and future life, both at work and at home.

Few of us are fortunate enough to have our own personal crest, so here is an opportunity for you to design yours!

Complete the *3 easy steps* crest on page 6, using the following guidelines:

Draw a picture in each of the sections to illustrate:

SECTION 1   How I like to spend my leisure time
SECTION 2   Something I did recently that I'm really proud of
SECTION 3   My greatest professional skill
SECTION 4   My greatest challenge for the next six months
BANNER   Write your own personal motto or slogan

This simple activity can be very useful to help you to start finding the key to unlock the answer to who you are and who you want to be. Why not take it out of the book, or photocopy it and put it on the wall where you're planning to work on *3 easy steps to the job you want*.

ACTIVITY 2

Self-esteem, stress and jobsearching

➡ Worry gives a small thing a big shadow.   Swedish proverb

Embarking on a jobsearch programme can be challenging, enjoyable and rewarding. For many people the career and life planning, which is part of our jobsearching process, is enlightening. It represents a removal of the blinkers – the first time they have looked at their own life, beyond the end of their nose! Jobsearching can also be very depressing because:

Jobsearches for positions in sales look like this:

no   no   no   no   no   no   no   no   no   no
no   no   no   no   no   no   no   no   no   no
no   no   no   no   no   no   no   no   no   no   YES

Jobsearches for positions in accounts look like this:

no   no   no   no   no   no   no   no   no   no
no   no   no   no   no   no   no   no   no   no
no   no   no   no   no   no   no   no   no   no   YES

Jobsearches for recent graduates look like this:

no   no   no   no   no   no   no   no   no   no
no   no   no   no   no   no   no   no   no   no
no   no   no   no   no   no   no   no   no   no   YES

Jobsearches for women-returners look like this:

no   no   no   no   no   no   no   no   no   no
no   no   no   no   no   no   no   no   no   no
no   no   no   no   no   no   no   no   no   no   YES

Jobsearches for administrators look like this:

no   no   no   no   no   no   no   no   no   no
no   no   no   no   no   no   no   no   no   no
no   no   no   no   no   no   no   no   no   no   YES

Whatever job you're searching for, jobsearches all look pretty similar! Sometimes there are more nos, sometimes not so many. Since few of us are good at taking NO, it's hardly surprising that a number of jobsearchers begin their jobsearch with a burst of initial enthusiasm which then turns to anxiety, self-doubt and depression.

REDUNDANCY

Perhaps you have noticed that I have avoided the term (redundant). A man cannot actually be redundant. He can be wrong for a job, his job can disappear from beneath him, his firm may have to contract for financial reasons, but I submit that he cannot actually be redundant. He is a man fresh out of a job, and he is a man who needs to be relocated in a new job. But he remains a man, not an empty space where one once was.

(Malcolm Levene, *The Observer*)

First let me apologise to women on Mr Levene's behalf – he seems to have failed to recognise their contribution to the workforce!

Whatever euphemisms people may use and whatever the organisational reasons, like 'downsizing', 'financial contraction' or 'mergers', in reality, the expression we all use as shorthand to describe what's happened is to say 'S/he's been made redundant'. My father was made redundant after 38 years as a coal miner, my brother-in-law was made redundant after 8 years as a security guard, and I was made redundant after 12 years in management.

There can be few people who do not know someone in their close group of friends or relatives who has not been 'made redundant'. Only when it happens to you can you begin to have an inkling of the effect it can have on a person's life.

Those who trivialise redundancy with statements like, 'Well of course if you haven't been made redundant at least once in your career, then you haven't been where the action is', probably haven't been there, or they'd be more sensitive.

Now I'm not going to insult you by offering trite and facile advice like 'Remember, tomorrow's another day' and 'Keep smiling and it'll all come good soon'.

It might be worth recognising, however, that you're not alone. You're not the only person who feels like they've received a kick in the ego from a size 12 boot. Common feelings are:

- SHOCK – not being able to appreciate what's happening.
- DENIAL – it's not really happening.
- ANGER – why me?
- LOST SELF-IMAGE – I've failed, my job has gone. I'll never get another.
- LOW SELF-ESTEEM – I'm worthless, I'm insecure.
- LOSS – of direction, colleagues, security and all of the 'comforts' which come from regular work.
- REJECTION – by the previous employer, by potential employers when they don't acknowledge applications, and by friends when they don't return phone calls.
- STIGMA – how do my friends and neighbours now feel about me? What will the children tell their school friends?
- LACK OF CONTROL – what if I contact all of my friends, identify lots of opportunities, make lots of applications, get interviewed, but still don't get a job?

Now all of that has cheered you up hasn't it! But you can take control. You now have a job. Your job is finding a new job, because it's unlikely that the job is going to come looking for you.

The success of your jobsearch will depend on both the quality and quantity of your efforts. Working through the activities in the book will help with the quality. You are in charge of the quantity, the number of hours you commit. Don't expect the telephone to start ringing just because you've sent your CV to three or four recruitment agencies.

Persistence does pay off. It is generally believed that when they get back into work most people get a job with more responsibility, greater job satisfaction and a higher salary than their previous job.

JOBSEARCHING IS STRESSFUL

Changing jobs is regarded by 'experts' as being one the most stressful things in our lives. In day-to-day life we need an amount of stress. To an extent the more stress we have then the better we work (see Figure 1). In other words, you need to strike the balance between challenge and having the resources to cope.

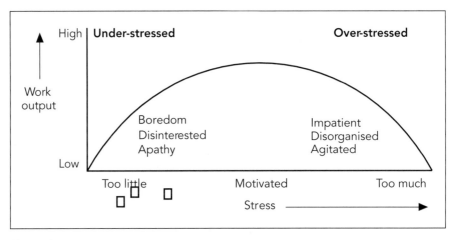

Figure 1

TO AVOID BECOMING OVER-STRESSED

- Take a proper break for lunch.
- Have a relaxation break for five minutes every hour or so.
- Take 20 minutes' exercise three times per week.
- Manage your time – organise your day so that you can spend some time relaxing with your friends and family.

● Have clear objectives – both long- and short-term ones – of what you want to achieve.

LOOK OUT FOR SIGNS OF BEING OVER-STRESSED

LEVEL 1

Over-energetic, over-enthusiastic, over-conscientious, overworked, feeling of uncertainty, doubts about coping.

Look out for:

Too busy to take time off, not knowing when to stop jobsearching, too little time spent with partner/family, frustrated with results.

LEVEL 2

Irritation, tiredness, anxiety, feeling of stagnation, blaming others.

Look out for:

Complaints about other people, unable to cope with pressure of handling a number of things at once, working long hours, not managing time efficiently.

LEVEL 3

General discontent, increasing anger/resentment, lowering of self-esteem, growing guilt, lack of emotional commitment, apathy.

Look out for:

Not enjoying life, extreme exhaustion, reduced commitment to jobsearching, reduced commitment to home.

LEVEL 4

Withdrawal, illness, feelings of failure, extreme personal distress.

Look out for:

Avoiding jobsearching activities, avoiding contact with other people, reluctance to communicate, isolation, physical illness, inability to get to sleep/early waking, alcohol or drug abuse.

IF YOU BECOME OVER-STRESSED

The following list offers some suggestions on how you can cope with stress.

- Try to analyse the problem logically, brainstorm solutions and pick the best option.
- Ask other people for advice.
- Spend time talking to other people (about anything!).
- Spend some time on your hobby.
- Take a weekend break.
- Eat proper, regular meals.
- Take some strenuous exercise.
- Reduce your intake of caffeine and alcohol.
- Make love with your partner.
- Indulge yourself in a hot bath, sauna or a massage.
- Socialise with friends.
- Pour out your problems to a good friend.
- Write all of your frustrations down on a piece of paper and then tear it up into the tiniest pieces you can.
- Have a good cry or a good shout in the privacy of your home.
- Be creative: Write poetry, sing, play a musical instrument.
- Start writing a book!

If it all seems as if it is becoming too much, the Samaritans will lend an ear – the number is in your telephone directory. Other useful numbers can be found at our website www.TheJobSearchersSuperstore.com.

Your local GP can also help. Indeed, many surgeries now have nurses who have received special training in counselling skills. They can be enormously useful in helping you to re-direct yourself.

Remember that you're not on your own. Your friends and family love and respect you, not for some job title you once held, but for the person you are.

ACTIVITY 3

Taking stock of my position

> ➡ Instead of saying that man is the creature of circumstance, it would be nearer the mark to say that man is the architect of circumstance. It is character which builds an existence out of circumstance. From the same materials one man builds palaces, another hovels; one warehouses, another villas; bricks and mortar are mortar and bricks until the architect can make them something else.   Thomas Carlyle

In this activity, which is in two parts, you will think about your life from the time you were born through to the time of your death. Most people find these exercises extremely powerful and enlightening.

If someone close to you has died recently, you may feel uncomfortable thinking about death and may wish to come back to this exercise at a later date. Other people have found, however, that the closeness of their loss has made the exercise even more meaningful.

Part I

0
_____
●   ●

The zero over the left dot represents your birth. Write the year you were born below it.

At what age do you think you will die? This is a difficult question but try to answer. Above the dot on the right of the line indicate your age at the time of your death. Write the year of your death below the dot.

Now put an 'x' on the line to show where you are now, between your birth and your death.

Look at your 'life line'.

What are your thoughts about the time that already has passed? What are your thoughts about the time that you have left? What are the three most important things you want to do in the next ten years? Write them below:

Goal A   _____

_____

Goal B   _____

_____

Goal C   _____

_____

Part II

It sounds morbid, but writing your obituary can help you to think clearly about your past and future life.

Write two obituaries for yourself: one if you had died yesterday and another if you were to die ten years from now.

You can:

● do the activity alone

● prepare your obituaries alone and then share them with your partner or a friend

● work with your partner or a friend to prepare obituaries for each of you.

The next page contains an outline of subjects you may want to include. This outline is intended to stimulate your thinking; modify the format if you wish.

Part II – Alternative: 'Suddenly I'm Famous'

If you feel uncomfortable at the thought of the above exercise try this alternative.

Imagine that you've suddenly become famous and tomorrow you'll be interviewed by a famous chat-show host such as Michael Parkinson or Sir David Frost. Use the sentences from the 'obituaries' to help you prepare for the interviewer's questions.

Now do the same for an interview ten years from now!

OBITUARIES

Complete the following sentences to write your own obituaries:

If I had died yesterday …

(Name)————————————died at the age of——————————. He/she was working on

becoming ———————————. (Name)——————————had always dreamed

of————————————. He /she had just completed——————————. The thing

he/she always wanted to do, but never did was ——————. (Name)——————————

will be remembered for ——————————. People will miss most ——————————

———.

He/she is survived by ——————————. The funeral will be ——————————

————————————————————. (Other information) ——————————

———.

If I were to die in 10 years' time …

(Name)————————————died at the age of——————————. He/she was working on

becoming ———————————. (Name)——————————had always dreamed

of————————————. He /she had just completed——————————. The thing

he/she always wanted to do, but never did was ——————. (Name)——————————

will be remembered for ——————————. People will miss most ——————————

———.

He/she is survived by ——————————. The funeral will be ——————————

————————————————————. (Other information) ——————————

———.

How do they compare? How will you make your 'ten years from now' come true?

ACTIVITY 4

My finances

➡ A wise man will make more opportunities than he finds.   Francis Bacon

For most people, their salary is their major form of income, yet many people identify their salary requirements in a totally subjective way. Often based on what recruitment ads say, we ignore the ones on lower salaries and notice only higher ones. We notice what contemporaries earn, what the next door neighbour earns, what our brother/sister earns, what our partner earns, etc., with little recognition of what our needs are!

If personal budgeting skills are one of your great strengths then this activity may be unnecessary. Others will find it very useful!

The exercise will help you to plan your finances and identify your target minimum salary, i.e. 2 x outgoings total, from the six-monthly financial planner, less any annual income.

If you are unemployed and are now the Managing Director of 'The Me Corporation' then you must do this exercise. After all, you wouldn't want to be employed by a company that didn't do proper financial planning, would you?

Gather together your bank statements, details of mortgage/rent, HP payments etc., and use the six-monthly financial planner (on page 19), to summarise your anticipated income and outgoings for the first month (use pencil).

Now repeat the exercise making your forecasts so that you build up a picture for the six-month period – this is a realistic period for many jobsearches.

Repeat the exercise at the end of the month and write how much you have spent in the 'actual' column. How are you doing against your budget? Do you need to re-forecast?

By carrying out this exercise you'll be able to anticipate those months when the gas bill, TV licence, car tax and car insurance all arrive at the same time! Also, you'll probably realise that with effective budgeting you can still indulge yourself in some of life's luxuries.

If you have got access to a computer and are familiar with using spreadsheets even better; simply use my headings to develop your own spreadsheet, or download a template from www.TheJobSearchersSuperstore.com.

FINANCIAL TIPS

These are primarily intended for unemployed jobsearchers but others may find the advice useful.

- Talk to your bank manager (check first to make sure there won't be a charge). They are financial experts and will be able to offer advice on budgeting and also advise on ways to invest a redundancy payment. In this transitionary period of your life, however, be very wary of investments where you can't get your money back quickly and without penalty. Longer term investments can be looked at when you've settled into the new job.

- Look for the simple ways of saving money – a magazine could cost you £3.00 in the newsagents, but can be read free at the local library. Going for a walk costs nothing and can be a great opportunity to think and plan.

- Talk to an independent financial adviser from a reputable company (beware, for many 'independent' and 'financial advisers' are misnomers, since they will have a vested interest in earning a sales commission). Talking to a financial adviser will help you to review your total financial picture, e.g. would it be advisable to take out additional short-term life assurance, now that you aren't covered by the company's policy? Is your will up to date? Should I leave my pension in my ex-company's fund or take a personal pension plan? Tread cautiously.

- Contact your Inland Revenue office – you may qualify for a refund.

- Sign on at the job centre and ask about benefits you are entitled to receive, including any job clubs, adult training and community work opportunities available. If you have been out of work for some time, an up-to-date reference from one of these organisations can be worth its weight in gold.

- Some money saving techniques can also generate a small income, e.g. as a child, my daughter Alison was keen on crafts, so she made jewellery and sold it at craft fairs. I like to keep up-to-date with management education, so I have taught a number of the Open University Business School courses. ('Teaching is learning twice'!) My friend Roland is keen on keep-fit, so he trained as a 'step' aerobics instructor and got free membership to his health-club, using his earnings from a weekly class to subsidise his other hobbies.

Six-monthly financial planner

BUDGET PERIOD _____ TO _____

(This form should be photocopied and enlarged)

Month	Budget £	Actual £	Budget £	Actual £	Budget £	Actual £	Budget £	Actual £	Budget £	Actual £	Budget £	Actual £
Budget vs Actual												
INCOME: Net Salaries												
Dividends Interest												
Other												
INCOME: TOTAL												
OUTGOINGS: Mortgage/Rent												
Loans/HP/Credit												
Household Services												
Insurances												
Transport												
Job Search												
House/Garden												
Food												
Holidays												
Social												
Dependants												
Personal												
Other												
OUTGOINGS: TOTAL												
Bank Opening Balances												
Bank Closing Balances												

INCOME
Net salaries = salary. Self/partner. Redundancy payments. Unemployment benefit. Social security payments.
Other = Tax refunds. Inheritance. Sale of assets. Bonuses.
OUTGOINGS
Mortgage/rent = Regular amount. Endowment assurance.
Loans/HP/credit cards = Total repayments. Items being paid off monthly.
Household services = Water rates. Council tax. Gas. Electricity. Telephone. TV licence/rent. Utilities.
Insurance = House and buildings. Life policies. Medical. House contents. Car(s). Accident/Disability. Pensions.
Transport = Car purchase. Fuel. Service/MOT. Road Tax. AA. RAC subs. Repairs/tyres. Bus fares.

Jobsearch = Secretarial services. Equipment. Postage. Paper/journals. Phone calls (Free at jobclub if 6mths unemployed).
House/garden = Maintenance. Alterations. DIY. Central heating. Furniture, etc. Garden tools. Plants. Sheds/fences. Domestic appliance maintenance/replacement.
Food = Family. Guests. Pets.
Holidays = Fares. Insurance. Hotels. Car hire. Entertainment. Gifts.
Social = Dining out. Entertainment. Clubs/equipment.
Dependants = Allowances. School fees. Gifts. Maintenance payments.
Personal = Clothes. Hobbies. Gifts. Church charity. Medical. Dental. Optician. Professional subs fees.
Other = Bank charges. Income gains tax (if taxable) contingencies.

- Clear out your loft and your garage – a trip to a car-boot sale as a seller can be enormous fun and you'll be amazed at what people will buy! But don't be unrealistic with your prices – remember people are looking for bargains.

- Lock away your credit cards! Being unemployed can be extremely expensive. Suddenly you have time on your hands and on your strolls down the high street you'll see lots of bargains you'd never seen before (you were at work!) – you didn't need them then, so do you really need them now?!

- If you have to sell a 'luxury' asset (e.g. your classic car, a boat or a piece of jewellery) then plan the sale well in advance so that you can obtain a realistic price. If you have to sell quickly, in desperation, you may accept a much lower price. Not only will you lose out financially, but it will depress you as well!

Lock away your credit cards!

DEBTS

- Tackle the problem immediately.

- Water, gas, telephone and electricity companies, etc., will often accept small instalments, as will credit card companies

- Contact the Social Security Hotline for free advice in office hours (number in phone book).

When you have predictable and regular income, you can often get away without paying too much heed to the outgoings!

When income is substantially reduced, with no immediate prospect of improvement, what you can take control of is the management of your outgoings.

ACTIVITY 5

Assessing my needs and wants in life

➡ Ethics, too, are nothing but reverence for life. That is what gives me the fundamental principle of morality, namely, that good consists in maintaining, prompting and enhancing life and that destroying, injuring and limiting life are evil.   Albert Schweitzer

STAGE 1

Look at the statements below. Tick the seven that are most important to you.

To feel I have stretched myself/fulfilled my potential. ☐

To make worthwhile things or provide a valued service. ☐

To be a successful parent. ☐

To be respected and acknowledged at work and home. ☐

To have a secure and untroubled life. ☐

To travel the world/Europe/country. ☐

To have as much pleasure as possible. ☐

To have no regrets in life. ☐

To enjoy love and companionship. ☐

To earn as much money as possible. ☐

To work overseas. ☐

To be free of other people's demands. ☐

To be a successful partner to my spouse. ☐

To do what I believe to be my duty. ☐

To help people less fortunate than I am. ☐

To become an acknowledged expert. ☐

To have power over other people. ☐

To become as famous as possible. ☐

Others. ☐

STAGE 2

Make notes of how you might be able to adapt your life to make sure that you are achieving your needs and wants.

Now rank those seven from most important (1) to least important (7).

1 _____
2 _____
3 _____
4 _____
5 _____
6 _____
7 _____

Keep these in mind when searching for your ideal job.

☺ My jobsearching dos ☺

_____
_____
_____
_____

☹ My jobsearching don'ts ☹

_____
_____
_____
_____

Use these notepads to summarise your learning points as you complete activities in *3 easy steps to the job you want.*

ACTIVITY 6

My own skills and knowledge

⟹ A man's best friends are his ten fingers.   Robert Collyer

If I asked you to list your skills and the knowledge that might be useful in your new job in the box below, you'd probably say, 'There's far too much room'!

Try it anyway.

> ### My skills and knowledge

What you have just listed is the tip of the iceberg.

You might say 'I've been too busy bringing up a family for the past ten years to develop any new skills', or, 'I've been too busy hitting sales targets …' or, 'Studying for my degree …' to build up additional knowledge.

As we go through life, we develop skills and knowledge, either wittingly or unwittingly.

In this activity you will identify the skills and knowledge you have built up through your life so that you can identify the transferable skills and knowledge to take into your new job.

Look at the three skills banks on the following pages and highlight or tick the skills you believe you have, are good at and enjoy doing. Then complete the 'knowledge reserves exercise' on the next page. These exercises do take some time to complete. Do some initial work and then come back to them. Brainstorm with your partner or a close friend. It is worthwhile!

Your transferable skills and knowledge bank is the vault containing the currency to obtain your next job.

As you work through these activities keep thinking of specific examples and how you can expand from the 'general' to the 'specific'. For example if one of your skills is 'writing', then a good example might be that report you did for senior management which swayed a board meeting or the short story you had published.

Time invested on this activity will reap its rewards when you write your CV, apply for jobs and attend interviews. You will find that you can easily and quickly identify those top skills and knowledge that you have and, importantly, articulate them to a potential employer, whether in writing or at an interview.

RETRAINING

'When we stop learning, we stop living.' One of the other things that may come out of this audit, is a recognition that there's a gap between where you are now and where you'd like to be: a 'training gap'. Think carefully about how you'd like to close that gap by taking additional training. Go to your library or search the internet, ask at the careers service, the job centre, your local college, to check out the options. Be aware of your own learning style. Some people can study alone and pass exams by reading a few books or taking a correspondence course. Others have to have the support of others. If you're out of work, you'll probably find that there are many courses that you can attend free of charge. Ask! And don't think you'll be the class dunce, just because you haven't studied for 20 years. You'll find that others on the course had the same fear. If you need some inspiration, to help you get over your anxiety, read Susan Jeffer's excellent book *Feel the Fear and Do It Anyway*.

SKILLS BANK

My transferable skills in dealing with people

I am good at and enjoy:

accepting	discovering	informing	pioneering	setting goals	washing
achieving	displaying	initiative	planning	sewing	winning
acting	dissecting	inspecting	playing	shaping	working
addressing	dramatising	inspiring	preparing	showing	writing
administering	drawing	instructing	presenting	singing to	
advising	driving	integrating	problem-solving	sketching	
amusing	empathising	interpreting	processing	speaking	
analysing	empowering	interviewing	promoting	studying	
arbitrating	encouraging	investigating	protecting	summarising	
arranging	enforcing	judging	providing	supervising	
assessing	enthusing	keep-fit	publicising	supplying	
auditing	establishing	leading	purchasing	symbolising	
budgeting	estimating	learning	questioning	synergising	
building	evaluating	lecturing	raising	synthesising	
caring	examining	listening	reasoning	systematising	
chairing	experimenting	maintaining	recommending	taking	
charting	explaining	making	reconciling	taking	
checking	expressing	inventories	recording	instructions	
classifying	financing	managing	recruiting	talking	
coaching	fixing	manipulating	referring	teaching	
communicating	following	mediating	rehabilitating	team-building	
conducting	founding	meeting	relating	telephoning	
consolidating	gathering	memorising	remembering	telling	
consulting	giving	mentoring	repairing	tending	
controlling	guiding	miming	reporting	testing	
conversing	handling	modelling	representing	tolerating	
co-ordinating	having	monitoring	researching	ambiguity	
coping	responsibility	motivating	resolving	training	
counselling	heading	negotiating	responding	translating	
creating	healing	observing	restoring	treating	
cultivating	helping	offering	retrieving	trouble-shooting	
debating	identifying	operating	risking	tutoring	
deciding	problems	organising	scheduling	umpiring	
defining	illustrating	originating	screening	understanding	
delivering	imagining	overseeing	selecting	understudying	
detailing	implementing	painting	self-	undertaking	
detecting	improving	performing	understanding	uniting	
developing	improvising	persuading	selling to	updating	
diagnosing	increasing	photographing	sensing	upgrading	
directing	influencing	piloting	serving	using	

SKILLS BANK

My transferable skills in dealing with things

I am good at and enjoy:

achieving	dispensing	illustrating	piloting	retrieving	typing
adapting	displaying	implementing	planning	reviewing	understanding
addressing	disproving	improving	playing	salvaging	undertaking
administering	dissecting	improvising	precision	scheduling	unifying
analysing	distributing	informing	predicting	sculpting	upgrading
arranging	drawing	innovating	preparing	selecting	using
assembling	driving	inspecting	prescribing	selling	utilising
auditing	editing	integrating	printing	sensing	washing
building	eliminating	interpreting	problem-solving	separating	weaving
carving	emptying	inventing	processing	serving	weighing
checking	enforcing	investigating	programming	setting	winning
chiselling	establishing	judging	projecting	setting-up	woodworking
classifying	estimating	keeping	promoting	sewing	working
cleaning	evaluating	lifting	proof-reading	shaping	writing
collecting	examining	logging	protecting	showing	
compiling	expanding	maintaining	providing	sketching	
completing	expediting	making	publicising	solving	
composing	experimenting	inventories	purchasing	sorting	
conserving	extracting	managing	raising animals	studying	
consolidating	fashioning	manipulating	reading	summarising	
constructing	feeding	manufacturing	realising	supervising	
controlling	filing	massaging	reasoning	supplying	
cooking	financing	memorising	receiving	symbolising	
co-ordinating	finishing	metalworking	recommending	synergising	
crafting	fixing	minding	reconciling	synthesising	
creating	forecasting	modelling	reconstructing	taking	
cultivating	founding	monitoring	recording	taking	
cutting	gathering	motivating	recruiting	instructions	
deciding	generalising	moulding	reducing	tending	
delivering	generating	navigating	referring	testing and	
designing	getting	observing	rehabilitating	proving	
detecting	giving	obtaining	remembering	thinking logically	
determining	growing plants	offering	rendering	tolerating	
developing	hammering	operating	repairing	ambiguity	
devising	handling	ordering	reporting	training animals	
diagnosing	having	organising	representing	transcribing	
digging	responsibility	originating	researching	translating	
directing	heading	overseeing	resolving	treating	
disassembling	identifying	painting	responding	trouble-shooting	
discovering	problems	photographing	restoring	tutoring	

SKILLS BANK

My transferable skills in dealing with concepts and information

I am good at and enjoy:

accounting	devising	responsibility	ordering	representing	thinking logically
adapting	diagnosing	hypothesising	organising	researching	tolerating
administering	digging	identifying	originating	resolving	ambiguity
analysing	discovering	problems	painting	responding	training
animating	displaying	illustrating	perceiving	restoring	transcribing
anticipating	disproving	imagining	piloting	retrieving	translating
ascertaining	dissecting	implementing	planning	reviewing	treating
assembling	distributing	improving	predicting	risking	trouble-shooting
assessing	diverting	improvising	preparing	scheduling	typing
auditing	dramatising	increasing	prescribing	searching	updating
budgeting	drawing	influencing	prioritising	selecting	understanding
calculating	editing	initiating	problem-solving	selling	undertaking
charting	eliminating	innovating	processing	sensing	unifying
checking	enforcing	inspecting	programming	separating	uniting
classifying	establishing	installing	projecting	sequencing	upgrading
collecting	estimating	instituting	promoting	setting-up	using
compiling	evaluating	integrating	proof-reading	shaping	utilising
completing	examining	interpreting	protecting	sharing	verbalising
composing	expanding	inventing	providing	sketching	visualising
computing	experimenting	investigating	publicising	solving	weighing
conceptualising	explaining	judging	purchasing	sorting	winning
conserving	expressing	keeping	questioning	storing	working
consolidating	extracting	learning	raising	studying	writing
constructing	filing	logging	reading	summarising	
controlling	forecasting	maintaining	realising	supplying	
copying	formulating	making	reasoning	symbolising	
creating	founding	managing time	receiving	synergising	
deciding	gathering	manipulating	recommending	synthesising	
decision-making	generalising	mediating	reconciling	systematising	
defining	generating	memorising	recording	taking	
delivering	getting	modelling	reducing	instructions	
designing	giving	monitoring	referring	telling	
detecting	guiding	observing	relating	tending	
determining	handling	obtaining	remembering	testing and	
developing	having	operating	reporting	proving	

Now that you have completed these skills banks, asterisk your 'top ten' on each page.

MY KNOWLEDGE RESERVES

It would be impossible to list an encyclopaedia of knowledge for you to use as a checklist, but thinking about different times in your life should trigger you to remember knowledge you have acquired.

Complete the chart below with subjects you know something about and enjoy.

Knowledge I have gained from:

School/college/ university e.g. Basic French	Work e.g. Auditing principles	Courses/ apprenticeships/ military e.g. Safety regulations
Reading: Books/ newspapers/magazines e.g. *Car Values*	Computers/video e.g. Career planning	Trial and error/self-study e.g. Marketing principles

ACTIVITY 7

My personality

➡ People have one thing in common; they are all different.   Robert Zend

Psychologists will probably argue for as long as people tread the earth as to whether our personality is 'caught' or 'taught' – whether we inherit it from our parents, or it develops as a result of our interaction with our environment. Whichever way we get it, we all have one! This exercise will help you to learn more about yours and about your personality 'type'.

Each of the paired blocks below contains two groups of words. Consider each block in turn and decide which list of words describes you best. There are no right answers and none of the groups of words is 'better' than any other. Do not choose how you would like to behave, but how you know you behave. You will probably find that some words in each of the paired blocks apply to you. Don't sit on the fence; choose which list is the better description of you. When you have made your choice circle the appropriate letter.

Circle your choice. Which describes you best?

E or I

E	I
Sociable	Composed
Expressive	Avoid crowds
Think out loud	Like one-to-one meetings
Like socialising in groups	Enjoy your own company
Uninhibited	Keep thoughts to yourself
Enjoy interacting with people	Entertain close friends in intimate groups

S or N

S	N
Factual	Conceptual
Operate from experience	Look for the 'big picture'
Practical	Innovative
Down-to-earth	Consider options
Pay attention to details	Enjoy new ideas
Make few errors	Future-oriented

T or F

T	F
Logical Rational Objective Analytical Fair Seek knowledge	Genuine Relationship-centred Harmonious Base decisions on personal values Compassionate Loyal and supportive

J or P

J	P
Determined Plan Organised Purposeful Set goals Decide quickly	Flexible Spontaneous Consider all of the options Adaptable Enjoy variety Like to keep options open

Now write the four letters you circled here (e.g. ENTP, my type) __ __ __ __.

This activity is based on basic personality characteristics and in the following pages you'll find a summary of your profile.

Clearly there are more than 16 (the number of combinations) 'kinds of people' in the world and I suggest that you now personalise your profile by crossing out words or expressions which do not describe you and, using a highlighter pen, pick out those that are definitely you.

This unique profile of you will be useful in helping you to communicate to employers the strengths that you can contribute to their organisation.

The section 'Others may be uneasy with' in the profiles on the following pages has been left blank. Try to see yourself the way others may see you and complete this section yourself in order to build a balanced view of your strengths and limitations. Discuss your profile with your partner or a close friend.

(*Author's note*: No explanation is offered here of the meanings of each of the letters associated with the 'questionnaire'. People trained in administering personality evaluations know what the letters stand for. It is far beyond the scope of this book to train you as a user of personality profiling instruments. Also, because of the simplicity of the exercise, it does not claim to be as accurate as the lengthy personality profiles carried out by psychologists. If you have access to this facility you will find it extremely useful. The type 'descriptors' e.g. fieldmarshal are taken from *Please Understand Me* by David Kiersey an excellent reference (at www.kiersey.com you can take a free 'type' analysis), as is *Life Types* by Sandra Hirsh, if you wish to find out more about personality types.)

Other profiling instruments are available through www.TheJobSearchersSuperstore.com as are more comprehensive descriptions of the following 16 types.

INTP – The architect

STRENGTHS
Creative
Handles change easily
Theoretical
Researches objectively
Idealist

Likes solving complex problems
Imaginative
Innovative
An 'idea' person
Has intellectual insight

AS A LEADER
Prefers to organise things, not people
Writes letters
Enjoys designing change

Enjoys pioneering concepts and ideas
Provides vision and scope

AS A TEAM MEMBER
Accepts the challenge of complex con-
    cepts
Is the 'idea' person
Is able to act as a reviewer of a project

Can incorporate change at any time
Offers creativity and innovation to a pro-
    ject

AT WORK
Needs quiet with occasional privacy
Wants flexibility
Enjoys challenges

Likes an unstructured workspace
Workspace may be cluttered

AT HOME/WITH FRIENDS
Is earnest and devoted parent
Uses low-key discipline
Likes a quiet home setting

Works at play
Prefers thinking games, e.g. bridge, chess
    etc.

OTHERS MAY BE UNEASY WITH

WHEN COMMUNICATING
Prefers written rather than verbal contact
Wants to discuss the 'big picture'
Likes discussing concepts and ideas

Can be hypothetical and verbose
Enjoys one-to-one contact

SUMMARY
Original
Future-oriented
Inquisitive
Speculative
Reserved

Global thought
Analytical
Independent
Determined
Uses abstract ideas

ENTP – The inventor

STRENGTHS

Alert to new possibilities
Entrepreneurial
Looks for better ways
Adapts to change
Enjoys learning new skills

Politically astute
Conceptual
Tactical
Like problem-solving

AS A LEADER

Is sociable and outgoing
Encourages innovation and creativity in
    others
Is open to constructive criticism

Relies on others to handle details
Develops models

AS A TEAM MEMBER

Makes strong initial contributions
Acts as the 'detonator' for the team
Incorporates new ideas

Sees the project reflected through people
Sees relationships between means and
    ends

AT WORK

Works best with independent people
Wants flexible management and guidelines
Needs challenge and reward for risk-taking

Enjoys group activities and gatherings
Likes 'start-ups' or re-organisations

AT HOME/WITH FRIENDS

Is high-spirited and outgoing
Enjoys group activities and gatherings
Wants a lively environment

Has an 'open-door' policy
Likes flexible relaxation time

OTHERS MAY BE UNEASY WITH

WHEN COMMUNICATING

Is quick and vocal
Enjoys debate
Is an interesting conversationalist

Is a motivating speaker
Is stimulated by new information

SUMMARY

Understands people
Enjoys new projects
Open-minded
Communicative
Curious and interested

Likes variety and action
Instinctive
Analytical
Enjoys a challenge
Enthusiastic and energetic

INTJ – The scientist

STRENGTHS

Highly practical
Systematic
Individualistic
Mentally quick
Committed

Independent
Resolute
Visionary
Self-motivated
Firm

AS A LEADER

Conceptualises and designs work models
Organises ideas into action plans
Plans strategies for new projects

Is tough-minded and decisive
Instils drive in self and others to attain
    goals

AS A TEAM MEMBER

Pushes for removal of obstacles
Has organisational vision
Is able to systemise goals

Implements new ideas
Streamlines complicated tasks and
    procedures

AT WORK

Likes intellectual challenges
Needs privacy for reflection
Wants efficient systems and procedures

Requires a certain amount of autonomy
Prefers a free hand for making decisions

AT HOME/WITH FRIENDS

Combines business with pleasure
Seldom leaves relaxation time to chance
Prefers well-planned activities

Is loyal and caring
Promotes independence in children

OTHERS MAY BE UNEASY WITH

WHEN COMMUNICATING

Communicates with specific purposes in
    mind
Believes that if people 'see it' they will
    understand it
Is detached and factual

Collects information visually
Uses logical structure

SUMMARY

Highly practical
Systematic
Individualistic
Mentally quick
Committed
Detached

Independent
Determined
Visionary
Self-motivated
Stable
Logical

ENTJ – The fieldmarshal

STRENGTHS
Enjoys being a leader
Provides structure
Highly analytical
Frank and to the point
Expects hard work

Sets high standards
Likes problem-solving
Admires strength in others
Uses helpful critiques
Prepares for all situations

AS A LEADER
Takes charge
Works for long-term goals
Follows structure and systems

Decisive and tough
Has priorities and deadlines

AS A TEAM MEMBER
Lays out a blueprint for success
Makes planning logical and workable
Accepts responsibility of explaining to
    others

Sees that the plan is fully implemented
Breaks project into elements

AT WORK
Wants to identify personally with the job
Prefers tough-minded colleagues
Prefers an orderly, controlled environment

Seeks both challenge and structure
Wants results to be valued

AT HOME/WITH FRIENDS
Organises and structures family events
Integrates family and career
Enjoys competition

Organises relaxation
Expects dedication and commitment from
    partners

OTHERS MAY BE UNEASY WITH

WHEN COMMUNICATING
Relies on the sixth sense
Looks for the 'structure' of information
Likes to debate an issue

Has a natural clarity of thought and speech
Is gifted with insights to language and its
    meaning

SUMMARY
Gregarious
Quick-witted
Controlled objectivity
Firm, yet fair
Efficient

Logical
Verbalises easily and well
Seeks challenge
Strategic

INFP – The questor

STRENGTHS

Creative

Persuasive

Encourages others

Has a sense of timing

Intuitive with people

Is genuinely enthusiastic

Awareness of time/history

Is gifted with language

A good listener

Is inspired by challenge

AS A LEADER

Prefers to facilitate rather than direct

Seeks out the self-starters

Subtle

Praises other people naturally

Is open to other people's ideas

AS A TEAM MEMBER

Emphasises need for group or organisational values

Presents high ideals and a goal of perfection

Stimulates co-operation

Senses the true needs of others

Is humanitarian

AT WORK

Works well alone

Prefers a company of high integrity

Needs time to reflect

Desires co-operative peers

Wants to be independent

AT HOME/WITH FRIENDS

Relates well to children

Allows others freedom and space

Is easygoing, flows with family needs

Schedules may be subject to change

Is protective of the home and family

OTHERS MAY BE UNEASY WITH

WHEN COMMUNICATING

Communicates best via the written word

Writes lyrically

Stresses importance of relationships

Moves people through use of words

Listens with sincere interest

SUMMARY

Idealist

Supporter of causes

Faithful

Searches for the truth

Noble

Honourable

Harmonious

Dedicated to duty

Gentle/polite

Committed

ENFP – The reporter

STRENGTHS

Originates projects

Anticipates needs

Stimulates potential

Concentrates intensely

At ease with others

Appreciates others' input

A perceptive observer

Looks on the bright side

Gives people 'space'

Sees people's potential

AS A LEADER

Knows how to motivate people

Promotes harmony

Conveys the overall value of work to others

Accepts new projects

Uses variety to stimulate others

AS A TEAM MEMBER

Brings enthusiasm and energy

Is a catalyst who brings people together

Initiates meetings and conferences

Gets things moving from the start

Provides new and interesting aspects and ideas

AT WORK

Enjoys working with colleagues

Prefers an open, friendly atmosphere

Needs variety and challenge

Enjoys an optimistic, idea-oriented workplace

Works best with warm, lively people

AT HOME/WITH FRIENDS

Is charming and gentle with others

Brings in surprise and pleasure

Is a devoted and flexible parent

Enjoys bringing people together

Seeks out unusual recreation

OTHERS MAY BE UNEASY WITH

WHEN COMMUNICATING

Is skilled with the written word

Stresses values

Wins trust through charm and flair

Listens intently

Involves other people in conversation

SUMMARY

Charismatic

Has zest for life

Discerning

Dynamic

Impromptu

Energetic and enthusiastic

Convincing

Intuitive with people

Versatile

Imaginative

INFJ – The author

STRENGTHS
Listens to others
Co-operative
Creative/innovative
Looks to the future
Determined

Puts integrity first
Consults with others
Patient in relationships
Gentle and accepting
Loyal

AS A LEADER
Is low key, yet determined
Matches people to the tasks
Wins co-operation from others

Supports causes and ideals
Inspires others to succeed

AS A TEAM MEMBER
Is an ambassador
Has insight into the needs of others
Works with integrity and consistency

Faces challenge to gain ideals
Helps others to achieve their goals

AT WORK
Needs solitude and room for concentra-
    tion
Seeks an easygoing environment
Likes room to be creative

Enjoys challenging and novel projects
Wants an organised and harmonious
    setting

AT HOME/WITH FRIENDS
Is concerned about home comforts
Develops long-term relationships
Enjoys a variety of interests and pursuits

Is a congenial companion
Is subtle in expressing affection

OTHERS MAY BE UNEASY WITH

WHEN COMMUNICATING
Is an elegant communicator, both written
    and oral
Prioritises the feelings of others
Considerate of others' views

Has a natural gift for language
Uses relationships as communication
    values

SUMMARY
Considerate
Highly committed
Calm and sensitive
Harmonious

Warm
Inspires others
Compassionate
Reserved
Accepts challenges

ENFJ – The pedagogue (instructor/educator)

STRENGTHS
Inspirational
Asks for commitment
Stimulates loyalty
Communicates values
Tactful

Has high standards
Uses an orderly approach
Wins others' respect
Gains co-operation
Responsive

AS A LEADER
Assigns tasks based on peoples' needs
Promotes group participation
Concerned about the feelings of colleagues

Prefers to know who is involved prior to
    decisions
Likes to adhere to the plan once it is
    underway

AS A TEAM MEMBER
Provides information about human issues
Relies on personal experiences and infor-
    mation
Protects the ideas and values of the
    organisation

Has an orderly approach
Maintains co-operation within the team

AT WORK
Desires an environment to benefit everyone
Expects surroundings to be settled and
    orderly
Likes a value-based, principled organisation

Enjoys harmony among co-workers
Wants a social, yet professional, feeling

AT HOME/WITH FRIENDS
Is romantic and devoted
Likes involved and caring relationships
Values harmony in the home

Family and responsibilities come first
Is community/service-oriented

OTHERS MAY BE UNEASY WITH

WHEN COMMUNICATING
Is openly talkative and social
Generates group involvement
Uses values and traditions as examples

Learns through interrelations
Perceptive

SUMMARY
Loyal
Diplomatic
Harmonious
People-oriented
Expressive

Responsible
Idealist
Supportive
Communicative
Concerned
Expressive

ESFJ – The seller

STRENGTHS
Gentle, yet firm
Fast, thorough worker
Quick to act
Promotes loyalty
Decisive

Unselfish with time
Excellent with people
Tirelessly assists others
Tactful with colleagues
Creates harmony

AS A LEADER
Leads through attention to individuals
Keeps people informed
Adds a 'personal touch'

Sets an example for hard work
Uses experience to support decisions and
   actions

AS A TEAM MEMBER
Promotes team efforts
Resolves conflicts
Is punctual and accurate with data

Respects rules and authority
Is in tune with the needs of
   people/employees

AT WORK
Likes goal-oriented colleagues
Prefers friendly, organised surroundings
Likes being where the action is

Needs colleagues who are appreciative
   and sensitive
Provides service within specified structure

AT HOME/WITH FRIENDS
Enjoys socialising and entertaining
Is the centre of an ordered family life
Is a provider for the future

Is warm, caring and committed
Is self-sacrificing and loyal

OTHERS MAY BE UNEASY WITH

WHEN COMMUNICATING
Is an entertaining conversationalist
Listens with understanding and sympathy
Appreciates others' viewpoints

Is a strong verbal communicator
Obtains information through the senses

SUMMARY
Gregarious
Supportive
Sympathetic
Co-operative
Popular

Respects tradition
Gracious
Personable
Conscientious
Helps friends

ISFJ – The conservator

STRENGTHS

Uses resources wisely
Knowledgeable
Just and fair
Task-oriented
Works tirelessly

Considerate of others
Personalises data
Accepts responsibility
Plans ahead
Simplifies information

AS A LEADER

Is consistent and orderly
Sets priorities around people
Is focused and detailed

Uses personal influence discreetly
Preserves traditional rules and procedures

AS A TEAM MEMBER

Is thorough and painstaking
Carries out detailed and routine tasks
Makes effective decisions and takes action

Personalises the goals and projects
Provides stability and follow-through

AT WORK

Prefers a secure working environment
Needs time to be alone
Wants order and routines

Appreciates accurate and conscientious
  colleagues
Enjoys direct physical involvement with
  work

AT HOME/WITH FRIENDS

Is devoted to the family
Enjoys traditional family activities
Maintains impeccable surroundings

Relaxes when work is finished
Values personal belongings

OTHERS MAY BE UNEASY WITH

WHEN COMMUNICATING

Uses examples and samples to communci-
  ate
Is direct and to the point
Is friendly and patient

Looks for clear-cut contrasts
Writes things down

SUMMARY

Sympathetic
Detailed and factual
Conscientious
Respects tradition
Sense of history
Impromptu

Down-to-earth
Sense of justice
Service-oriented
Meticulous with detail
Practical and organised

ESFP – The entertainer

STRENGTHS
A keen observer
A 'do it' person
Optimistic
Enthusiast
Advocates harmony

Accepts people for who they are
Generous with time
Sociable
Understands most people

AS A LEADER
Handles crises well
Facilitates the interaction of people
Promotes good will and teamwork

Is attentive to the expectations of others
Encourages agreement and compromise

AS A TEAM MEMBER
Brings in enthusiasm and co-operation
Offers action and excitement
Does it now – doesn't linger

Takes account of the needs of people
Supports the organisation loyally

AT WORK
Likes an energetic, yet easygoing
  atmosphere
Prefers to focus on present realities
Prefers adaptable and lively colleagues

Likes the centre of action to be around
  people
Wants attractive surroundings

AT HOME/WITH FRIENDS
Is generous to others
Enjoys a beautifully decorated home
Is sentimental and enjoys pleasing others

Is sociable and spontaneous
Likes a varied and busy day

OTHERS MAY BE UNEASY WITH

WHEN COMMUNICATING
Is a straightforward communicator
Uses a simple and sensitive approach
Enjoys talking

Stimulates conversation
Relates today's situations to people

SUMMARY
Open and outgoing
Pleasant
Co-operative
Positive and upbeat
Empathetic

People-oriented
Tolerant
Realistic
Quick to act
Adaptable

ISFP – The artist

STRENGTHS

Receptive to others
Generous with time
Open-minded
Generates trust in others
Respects others' feelings

Unconditionally kind
Eternal optimist
Solves problems
Understanding and trusting

AS A LEADER

Praises and encourages
Monitors group performance
Is adaptable and co-operative

At hand in a crisis
Is able to utilise the strengths of others

AS A TEAM MEMBER

Is co-operative
Brings focus to people's needs
Understands the need for teamwork

Builds systems around productive people
Provides service to a project

AT WORK

Needs a private, unconfined space
Wants compatible colleagues
Desires flexibility to be productive

Likes an aesthetic work environment
Is concerned about people's actions

AT HOME/WITH FRIENDS

Enjoys private leisure time
Is personable and humorous
Takes time for simple pleasures

Needs to maintain relationships
Enjoys solitary pursuits

OTHERS MAY BE UNEASY WITH

WHEN COMMUNICATING

Is in tune with the needs of others
Prefers clam, controlled conversations
Looks for meaning in people's actions and
    words

Listens, before speaking
Likes quiet, considerate colleagues

SUMMARY

Gentle and considerate
Quiet disposition
Has an inner intensity
Can act spontaneously
Is in touch with reality

Unpretentious
Sensitive to others
Artistic
Unassuming
Co-operative and balanced

ESTJ – The administrator

STRENGTHS

Plans ahead

Declares views openly

Uses experience

Good organiser

Follows through

Meets deadlines

Prompt decision-maker

Respects authority

Tough-minded

Manages and controls

AS A LEADER

Is direct and to the point

Applies past experiences to resolve problems

Uses rewards with employees

Takes charge

Firm, yet open to ideas

AS A TEAM MEMBER

Works well with policies and procedures

Is effective at controlling time spent on a
project

Understands the importance of full
co-operation

Is prepared to act when called upon

Uses a systematic approach to a challenge

AT WORK

Enjoys being in charge

Likes to work alongside dedicated colleagues

Prefers defined projects

Prefers stable and predictable
surroundings

Likes to work with, and through, people

AT HOME/WITH FRIENDS

Is community-minded

Is prudent and conservative

My home is my castle

Mixes business with pleasure

Has strong family ties

OTHERS MAY BE UNEASY WITH

WHEN COMMUNICATING

Is an effective verbal communicator

Is a good sounding board for others

Is crisp and direct

Communicates with facts

Wants outlines rather than details

SUMMARY

Deals in reality

Goal-oriented

Responsible

Stable

Systematic

Conscientious

Organiser

Thorough

Decisive

Logical and objective

ISTJ – The trustee

STRENGTHS

Knows the rules

Follows guidelines

Likes structure

Dependable

Accepts responsibility

Adapts to new routines

Takes charge

Team-oriented

Puts work before play

Meets deadlines

AS A LEADER

Sets the standard for others

Is goal-oriented and expects others to be

Controls resources and costs

Is direct and succinct

Supports existing systems, structures and
  standards

AS A TEAM MEMBER

Organises and plans

Follows schedules

Meets deadlines

Respects traditions and rules

Takes responsibility for the project

AT WORK

Plans the work and works to the plan

Wants details

Likes a task-oriented, quiet environment

Prefers involvement

Expects work to be orderly

AT HOME/WITH FRIENDS

Is trustworthy and dedicated

Committed to the family

Expects rules to be adhered to

Is a pillar of strength

Is conservative

OTHERS MAY BE UNEASY WITH

WHEN COMMUNICATING

Likes visuals – flowcharts, diagram and
  graphs, etc.

Direct and to the point

Is logical and sequential

Respects agendas

Relates to experience

SUMMARY

Thorough

Factual

Tangible

Consistent

Committed

Reliable

Reserved

Orderly

Systematic

Down-to-earth

ESTP – The promoter

STRENGTHS

Straightforward
Handles risks
A negotiator
Initiates
Responds quickly

Results-oriented
Remembers data and facts
Takes action
Mediates problems
A realist

AS A LEADER

Is direct
Is attentive at meetings
Handles problems quickly

Takes charge in emergencies
Uses persuasion to speed things along

AS A TEAM MEMBER

Acts as a go-between in negotiations
Adapts to working with all types
Supports projects with data and facts

Is able to adapt to last-minute changes
Likes being the trouble-shooter

AT WORK

Wants minimal bureaucracy
Includes time for fun while working
Wants an attractive work environment

Likes to master technical problems
Desires result-oriented colleagues

AT HOME/WITH FRIENDS

Is active with friends and family
Enjoys both personal and group activities
Has wide outside interests

Is a fun-loving charmer
Likes impromptu projects and parties

OTHERS MAY BE UNEASY WITH

WHEN COMMUNICATING

Uses both oral and visual communication
Is personable and engaging
Enjoys discussing plans and operations

Likes a 'real' debate
Is perceptive of body language

SUMMARY

Easygoing
Prepared for action
Lively and quick
A realist
Resourceful

Spontaneous
Versatile
Entertaining
Persuasive
Alert

ISTP – The Artisan

STRENGTHS

Receptive to others
Calm in a crisis
Trusting
Fount of knowledge
Dextrous

Has technical insight
Risk-taker
Trouble-shooter
Gets things done
Action-oriented

AS A LEADER

Wants subordinates to follow their example
Manages work and people with minimal controls
Is able to respond to emergencies

Likes people to build action groups
Seeks new ideas and methods

AS A TEAM MEMBER

Enjoys compiling relevant technical data
Has a sense of priority to achieve a goal

Is able to adapt to last-minute changes
Will work within specific guidelines
Wants to be involved in new projects

AT WORK

Likes project-oriented operations
Likes to work with action-oriented people
Wants to be involved

Likes dealing with things rather than people
Prefers flexible rules and procedures

AT HOME/WITH FRIENDS

Is private and protective of family
Is responsive and realistic
Is attentive to the needs of others

Is relaxed and easygoing
Enjoys repairing things for the family

OTHERS MAY BE UNEASY WITH

WHEN COMMUNICATING

Likes talking to people one to one
Is direct, yet open with others
Seeks essential facts

Likes technical data
Learns by doing

SUMMARY

Reserved
Factual
Logical
Adaptable
Independent

Practical
Down-to-earth
Analytical
Prudent
Spontaneous

ACTIVITY 8

What do I want from my job?

➡ He that hath a trade hath an estate; he that hath a calling hath an office
of profit and honour.   Benjamin Franklin

Q Why do you go to work? **A** To earn a living. But it goes way beyond that. Money is important – but it isn't everything. Research has shown that, while earnings are important, people expect a good deal more from their jobs. A recent survey by the Industrial Society showed interest/enjoyment, job security and a sense of accomplishment were more important than basic pay for most people. You are not 'most people', though. Study the following and rank them 1 for the factor most important to you, 15 for the factor least important to you.

Job factor	My importance ranking: 1–15
Advancement opportunities	
Basic pay	
Credit for a job well done	
Flexible hours	
Fully utilising skills/talents	
Go ahead employer	
Having a say	
Interest/enjoyment	
Job security	
Learning new skills	
Physical working conditions	
Sense of accomplishment	
Skilled management	
Sufficient help/equipment	
Working for a boss you respect	

When you're jobsearching check to make sure that at least your top five job factors will be satisfied. Don't leap on the salary bandwagon. Yes, it is important but it's not everything.

The grass MAY be greener – but then again it may not. According to a recent international survey in which 19,000 workers were interviewed, only one out of every three of Britons said they enjoy work. The unhappy ones blamed longer hours, commuting time and poor job security for their dissatisfaction. The picture wasn't that different in other industrialised countries with French, German, Russian and Japanese workers expressing a similar level of discontent.

If you're thinking about a career change ask yourself: What am I running away from? What am I running towards?

Imagine you're a personnel manager in a small company. You love the close contact you have with everyone. Your boss, the managing director, trusts and respects the quality of your work and gives you a wide amount of latitude to make decisions. She gives you fair appraisals and makes sure that you're always being stretched a little, by involving you in lots of nice project work. It's also nice and handy having only a 20-minute drive to work. You love your job.

A telephone call from a head-hunter and a couple of interviews land you a job on £3,500 per year more and a company car? Yippee! OK, you'll have to put up with an hour and a half drive into the city each morning. But it's worth it, because now you're the compensation and benefits specialist for 'Huge International' … or is it? You're locked in an office on the tenth floor, surrounded by computer terminals, a library of policies and procedures and computer printouts. You rarely see your boss. You can do the job standing on your head. You're bored to tears. You're ready to leave after six months, but all of a sudden the jobs have evaporated!

As you identify potential job opportunities check, as far as you can, to make sure that your top five or six job factors will be satisfied – after all, you wouldn't want to be starting all over again in another six months, would you?

WHY PEOPLE RESIGN – THE SIX MOST COMMON REASONS

There are six main reasons why people resign and more than just one of these reasons is usually involved:

- **Initial expectations mis-match:** The interviewer fails to describe the position accurately. Initial expectations do not match up to the reality of working.

- **Lack of communication:** Normal work pressures often make communication difficult. People may feel forgotten, they think they are being given the 'mushroom treatment', always kept in the dark while up to their waists in manure. Isolation or uncertainty breed insecurity, apathy and cynicism. People resign out of frustration.

- **Challenge:** People hate being in a rut, feeling that they have outgrown their job.

- **Lack of recognition:** How many times have you felt your hard work and commitment have not even been recognised, let alone rewarded?

- **Training and development:** If a person is not developing and being stretched within his or her job, then the company is providing a job rather than a career. Training adds 'value' to the individual. It also makes a person appreciate the company more. It shows the company has a commitment to its people.

- **Culture fit:** Every company has its own style or culture. Sometimes there is a mis-match between a person and the company's culture and the employee leaves.

How does your target company measure up to these points? Use the following checklist to assess its suitability. If you cannot tick all six, ask yourself if it's the right company for you.

Target company checklist

- **Expectations**
  Do I/they know what I'm/they are letting myself/themselves in for?   ☐

- **Communication**
  Are channels of communication obvious? Do they work?   ☐

- **Challenge**
  Am I going to be stretched?   ☐

- **Recognition**
  Will my contribution be recognised?   ☐

- **Training and development**
  Will I get any?   ☐

- **Culture**
  Do I like their style? Will I fit in?   ☐

ACTIVITY ⑨

Career/life interface

⇒ Occasionally in life there are those moments of unutterable fulfilment which cannot be completely explained by those symbols called words. Their meanings can only be articulated by the inaudible language of the heart.   Martin Luther King, Jr.

Jobsearching and career planning isn't something you can do in isolation. The decisions you make about your career impact on your life outside work, just as your activities outside work impact on your career, e.g. business travel is a normal part of organisational life. In considering a new job, you may want to determine how much travel is involved and what effect that will have on your personal and family life. Having to work shifts changes the pattern of people's lives completely.

At the same time, it may be necessary to make certain compromises between your career and personal development. Only you can decide exactly what compromises you are prepared to make.

No matter how challenging and satisfying a job is, it cannot meet all of your needs for personal growth and development. You have a rewarding life outside work as well. Successful people are usually well-balanced, with a number of outside interests. A full leisure and family life refreshes them to perform more effectively at work and allows them to bring a broader scope of vision to their jobs.

This activity enables you to review how well you balance the different areas of your life. You will then set yourself goals for how you want to balance your life in future.

The activity is in three stages.

STAGE 1

Imagine that the circle on page 54 is a 'pie' representing your life during the last year. Divide the pie into slices representing how you currently (or most recently when working) allocate(d) your waking time – into the 'slices' of your life. Use any division that is meaningful to you. Possible labels for your slices could be:

- attending church
- community and professional activities
- community and professional activities
- personal development
- professional development
- professional development

- continuing education
- education
- entertainment
- financial management
- fun
- hobbies
- household maintenance
- surfing the Net

- reading
- relationships
- shopping
- spending time with friends
- sports
- watching TV
- work

The size of each slice should represent the amount of time you spend on each activity. For example, if you spend/spent half your waking hours on work, that should account for half of the circle.

My 'life pie' for the last year

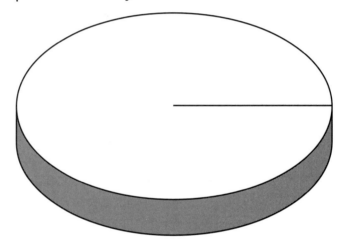

STAGE 2

Make a few notes as you answer these questions. Ask yourself:

- Am I satisfied with the way I balance my life?
- What parts are out of balance?
- What is the impact of this neglect on myself and those who are close to me?
- What activities do I spend too much time on and what can be done about it?

Now slice your 'ideal pie' as you would like to spend your time. To remind you, possible labels for your slices could be:

- attending church
- children
- community and professional activities
- continuing education
- education
- entertainment
- financial management
- fun
- hobbies
- household maintenance
- surfing the Net

- personal development
- physical fitness
- professional development
- reading
- relationships
- shopping
- spending time with friends
- sports
- watching TV
- work

My ideal 'life pie'

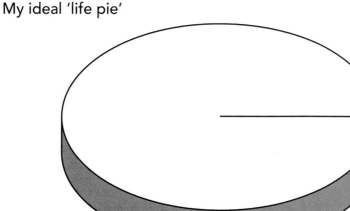

STAGE 3

Complete the summary and action plan table. Write your aims in the left-hand column, e.g. 'I want to become fitter.' In the right-hand column state what you intend to do about your aims, e.g. 'Join an aerobics club', to turn your aim, into achievable goals.

Time goals and action plan

Goals	Action plan: What I'm going to do
I want to spend more time:	
I want to spend less time:	

NB If you can use a spreadsheet such as Microsoft Excel, why not use the headings for Steps 1 and 2 to plot your life pie charts on your PC?

ACTIVITY 10

My values

➡ For anything worth having one must pay the price; and the price is always work, patience, love, self-sacrifice.　John Burroughs

Values – what we care about – guide our actions and determine how we experience the world. Values change as we grow older, to reflect experiences and stages in our lives and careers. As children, our most important value may be winning the love of our parents. As we grow and mature, new values such as autonomy, achievement and the need of self-approval become important. Parenthood may shift the emphasis once again.

It can be easy to lose touch with what is important to us in the process of managing our day-to-day activities. Also, because many of us do not stop to reflect on our values, we fail to challenge the way we see the world.

Understanding your values can help you in:

● selecting the kind of position and work to suit you

● understanding the kind of people you most like to associate with

● allocating your finances and time to achieve the greatest personal satisfaction.

This activity will help you to increase your awareness of what is most important to you and what you want out of your life and your career.

Read the values on page 58. If necessary, modify or re-write them to make them more meaningful to you. Add any values you feel are missing.

Mark each value in terms of its importance to you as high, medium or low (regardless of how well you are currently satisfying that value in your life). Try to allocate roughly one-third of the values to each category.

Complete the exercise as you think about these values right now. And remember, it's not what you think the world wants you to think, but what **you** value.

For most people the initial reaction is to place a high ranking on all of the values. Try to prioritise what are your most important and least important values at this time in your life.

WHAT I REALLY VALUE IN LIFE

	Importance		
	High	Medium	Low
Accomplishment: To achieve: to reach the top			
Affection: To obtain and share warmth, caring, companionship with family, friends, colleagues			
Affiliation: To be accepted and liked by others			
Autonomy: To direct my priorities and schedules			
Challenge: To have interesting, challenging work			
Competence: To be respected for my ability			
Expertise: To be a respected authority			
Family: To spend time with my family and to have meaningful relationships			
Growth: To maximise my full potential; to be constantly learning, changing and developing			
Health: Physical health, fitness			
Integrity: To have the courage of my convictions; to be honest, to uphold my beliefs			
Leadership: To influence and direct others			
Location: To live where I want to live			
Money: To be financially successful			
Pleasure: To have fun; to enjoy life and work			
Recognition: To have status and the respect of others			
Security: To achieve a secure financial situation			
Service: To help other people; to contribute to the well being of others; to help improve society			
Spiritual: Inner harmony; to be at peace with myself and live by my moral and ethical beliefs			
Other values:			

When you have completed this section move to the next page.

SUMMARISING MY VALUES

Use this page to analyse how your values are currently being satisfied and what you must do in the future.

At this time in my life my five most important values are:

1. _____   2. _____   3. _____   4. _____   5. _____

My values which **must be** satisfied in my:

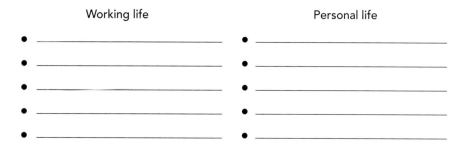

Working life	Personal life
• _____	• _____
• _____	• _____
• _____	• _____
• _____	• _____
• _____	• _____

Ways in which I may be able to achieve greater satisfaction of my values in my working life are:

_____

_____

_____

_____

Ways in which I may be able to achieve greater satisfaction of my values in my personal life are:

_____

_____

_____

_____

My life's achievements

➡ They are able because they think they are able.   Virgil

Do you keep a 'brag box', as my friend Tony calls it? My own is a bursting box file … and as I'm writing this, I'm reminding myself that it is overdue for updating! I can't think of a better name than the one Tony uses, so we'll call it a brag box! I'm talking about a collection point for documents logging your achievements through life.

When you come to complete your CV, or find you've got one hour to fill in an application form in order to catch the post, you'll be glad of your brag box!

Do you keep a brag box?

Some of the things to include in your brag box (either as copies or originals) could be:

Birth certificate	Exam certificates
Marriage certificate	Degree(s)
Children's birth certificates	Examples of your work
Passport (for no.)	CV
Driving licence	Personality and other evaluations
Membership certificates for professional institutes	Historical salary data
	Performance rankings, e.g. sales figures
Licences to practise	Special thank-you letter from your boss or the MD!
Career evaluations	
Testimonials	Sports certificates
Appraisals	This book!

As well as the functional aspect, you'll find your brag box useful for cheering you up on a wet Tuesday afternoon, when you feel as if you've telephoned everyone in the world and 'They're all in meetings'! But don't get too lost down memory lane … the meetings do end!

If you haven't got a brag box start one now!

PUTTING YOUR BRAG BOX TO WORK

Identifying your achievements will help you to realise that you have a wide variety of skills. You can use the information you develop in this exercise in CV presentation, completing application forms and job interviews.

Use the information in your brag box to help you to identify achievements you are proud of. Pick:

- four from the past two years
- three from the five-year period before that.

Now think about the skills you used and what made your achievements so satisfying. The following phrases are often used in describing achievements:

Work achievements

Improved productivity in _____ by _____.

Successfully convinced (my manager, subordinates, etc.) to _____.

Developed (introduced, designed, etc.) a new (method/system, etc.)
for_____ resulting in _____.

Motivated subordinates by _____.

Detected a serious error in (a procedure, filing system, report etc.)
and _____.

Improved technological process (service, etc.) by _____.

Successfully arranged and ran a meeting on _____.

Changed _____.

Improved quality control in _____ by _____.

Successfully arranged and ran a meeting on _____.

Initiated and implemented a (programme campaign, process, etc.)
to _____.

Increased market share of _____.

Non-work achievements

Created (managed, ran, etc.) a fund-raising campaign for (name of charitable, athletic or artistic activity/group).

Successfully counselled, advised, helped a friend.

Organised (co-ordinated, etc.) a charitable drive.

Successfully renovated my home myself.

Established (acted as secretary of) a professional association (social, athletic club, etc.).

Acted as a member of a committee or chaired a committee.

Did (oversaw) the decorations for _____.

As (a founding member of a local organisation) created a campaign
to _____, successfully raised funds for _____ , etc.

Organised a day trip to _____,
for a group of _____ (mothers and toddlers).

Having identified your achievements complete the tables on the following pages
I have included an example to help you to start the process.

Example

Achievement	Skills used	What made the achievement satisfying?
Co-ordinated sponsored run	Conceived the campaign	Managing
Enlisted six volunteers to assist in organising the campaign	Managing others	Planning the campaign
Informed local newspaper to generate publicity	Motivating others	Running meetings
Ran four meetings with volunteers	Planning	Contributing to something I believe in
Co-ordinated the volunteers by assigning tasks	Organising	The results – £5000!
Developed plan to go to the schools to inform people about the run and enlist volunteers	Delegating tasks	Being recognised
Got 200 people to participate in the run	Running effective meetings	Being in the limelight
	Public relations – selling the campaign	
	Persuading people to participate	

ACHIEVEMENTS FROM THE PAST TWO YEARS

Achievement	Skills used	What made the achievement satisfying?
Achievement No. 1		
Achievement No. 2		
Achievement No. 3		
Achievement No. 4		

ACHIEVEMENTS FROM THE PAST SEVEN YEARS

Achievement	Skills used	What made the achievement satisfying?
Achievement No. 5		
Achievement No. 6		
Achievement No. 7		

ACTIVITY (12)

Seeking feedback from others

⮕ O wad some Pow'r the giftie gie us
To see oursels as others see us!
It wad frae mony a blunder free us,
And foolish notion.

Robert Burns

All the exercises so far have concentrated on self-analysis. The next step is to move from self-analysis to gather information about how other people see you. No matter how honest and thoughtful you have been, we all have blind spots! Others may point to weaknesses we are unaware of, or more commonly, strengths and abilities we have underestimated.

Clearly no two people will see you in exactly the same way. Neither is it true that other people will always see you more accurately than you see yourself. By talking to people whose opinion you value, you will develop a clearer picture of yourself.

Whose opinion do I value?

Write down the names of people whose opinions you value. These may be your:

- current manager
- colleagues
- friends
- partner

- previous manager
- subordinates
- family members
- neighbours

Ideally they:

- have observed you in different situations
- know you well and how you react to different situations
- have your best interests at heart
- are perceptive.

People whose opinions I value are:

_____

_____

_____

WHAT SORT OF FEEDBACK DO YOU WANT?

The feedback you solicit from each person will, of course, depend on your relationship with them.

Friends and family can provide you with important feedback in such areas as your interpersonal skills; decision-making style; communication skills; ease of social interaction; some of your personality characteristics; how well you plan; how well organised you are, etc.

Don't discount this feedback. If you can do something well at a party or at home, then the chances are that you could also do it well at work. Similarly, weaknesses seen at home are probably applicable to work as well. For example, if your partner tells you that you don't listen very well, or that you have difficulties managing your temper, then you probably have similar difficulties in the work environment!

Your manager and other work contacts (current or past) are obviously an important source of information. Some questions you may want to ask:

- What do you see as my major skills? Strengths?
- What do you see as my major development areas?
- How can I improve how I am seen by others?
- What areas should I try to improve ?
- What kinds of job do you think I can realistically aspire to over the next few years?
- Are you aware of any jobs that I would do well?
- How realistic do you think my career goals are, based on what I've told you?
- What training and/or development do you think I need to attain these goals?
- What are the possible obstacles to me accomplishing my goals?

● What do you see as the key things I could do to improve my chances of achieving my goals?

Remember, people like to be asked for their opinions. Some may surprise you with their candour.

Be prepared to feel a little down when they talk to you about your limitations, and be prepared for the red glow of embarrassment which will come when they start to sing your praises!

If the people you have asked are unused to giving this sort of feedback they may appreciate some notice of your questions. In addition, giving them a copy of the page from the next activity, 'Selecting a mentor – Giving feedback', will help.

Based on the feedback you have received you may wish to develop new skills and abilities. This may be particularly relevant if you're returning to work after a break, e.g. bringing up a family, looking after an elderly relative or full-time education. Some ways of doing this are:

● Working with someone

● Taking a training course

● Continuing your education

● Taking a developmental assignment

● Enlarging your position by taking on responsibilities which will stretch you

● Joining a club or society, especially as a committee member

● Reading

(Clearly some of the options above are only available to people who are currently in work. If you aren't, think laterally to try to identify alternatives, e.g. work placement with a local employer.)

If you were to develop new skills and abilities:

What skills, knowledge or abilities are they?

_____

_____

_____

How will you do this?

_____

_____

_____

In what ways might you want to develop yourself?

_____

_____

_____

How can you do that?

_____

_____

_____

ACTIVITY 13

Selecting a mentor

> There is no such thing as a 'self-made' man. We are made up of thousands of others. Everyone who has ever done a kind deed for us, or spoken one word of encouragement to us, has entered into the make-up of our character and of our thoughts, as well as our success.   George Matthew Adams

Do you have someone whom you can use as a sounding board for your ideas?

As you develop your career, life and jobsearching ideas and plans, you will find it very beneficial to 'bounce' them off someone else. They'll be far more meaningful when you explain them to someone else.

WHO SHOULD YOU ASK?

Ask someone who knows you well and whose opinion you value. You will probably find it best not to use your partner. Please do not misunderstand me – I'm not advising you should exclude your partner; not at all. But they may not be able to 'see the wood for the trees', because of their emotional involvement. If you have access to a professional counsellor you will find it very useful. If not, don't despair. What about a favourite uncle or aunt? An old school/college/university friend? A current or previous work colleague? A neighbour? A fellow member of a sports or social club?

What qualities should a mentor have?

- A mentor should be a good listener – you should do most of the talking.
- A mentor should be genuine – someone who has a genuine interest in you.
- There should be mutual respect as it is important that you talk as equals.
- A mentor should be in touch with reality – if your dreams and goals become unrealistic they should help you back to earth gently.

Remember, your mentor is not your adviser: a good mentor won't begin sentences with 'If I were you I would …' or, 'Why don't you …'. It's your job to develop the ideas and use your mentor as a 'testing ground'.

A simple test to see if they are the right person may be to ask yourself, 'Would I choose them as my boss?'

WHEN SHOULD YOU MEET?

It is a good idea to have regular meetings for an hour or two weekly or fortnightly.

WHAT ARE THE BENEFITS?

You will find that your plans are modified, refined and more realistic. And all it will cost you is a box of chocolates, a special thank-you at Christmas or a couple of beers!

You may wish to give a photocopy of the next page to your mentor.

SELECTING A MENTOR – GIVING FEEDBACK

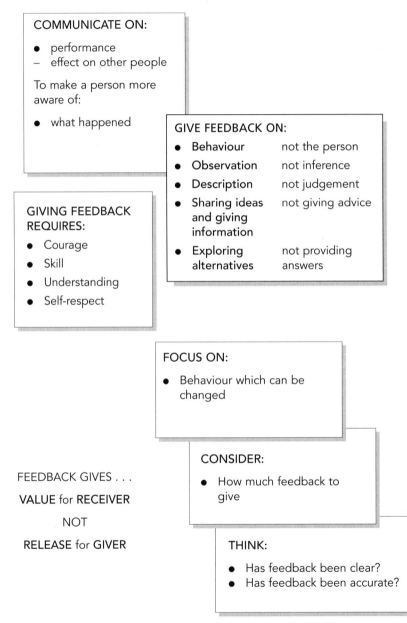

COMMUNICATE ON:

- performance
- effect on other people

To make a person more aware of:

- what happened

GIVE FEEDBACK ON:

- Behaviour — not the person
- Observation — not inference
- Description — not judgement
- Sharing ideas and giving information — not giving advice
- Exploring alternatives — not providing answers

GIVING FEEDBACK REQUIRES:

- Courage
- Skill
- Understanding
- Self-respect

FOCUS ON:

- Behaviour which can be changed

FEEDBACK GIVES . . .

VALUE for **RECEIVER**

NOT

RELEASE for **GIVER**

CONSIDER:

- How much feedback to give

THINK:

- Has feedback been clear?
- Has feedback been accurate?

Step 2

WHERE AM I GOING?

Establishing a new strategic direction

INTRODUCTION TO STEP 2

There is only one success – to be able to spend your life in your way.

Christopher Morley

Wouldn't it be wonderful if you could work through a few exercises to help you know more about yourself, decide on a new career direction, pick up the newspaper, make a few phone calls and, hey presto!, get a new job.

Life isn't like that and I'm sure you didn't need me to point it out!

So far in this book the principal point of focus has been you. But you don't exist in a vacuum. The job you want is out there in the real world.

We are now going to switch to take a more panoramic view. You will still be a major part of the picture and we will start to summarise some of the things you have learned about yourself in Step 1.

We will also consider the external environment – what jobs could you do? What are good bets for the future and the not so good bets?

I'm not going to offer you a list of jobs, though! If I did there wouldn't be space for anything else in the book! Indeed, we would need an extra 20 or 30 volumes.

Through your research activities you will identify job opportunities. Many of which you haven't even thought of so far!

ACTIVITY 14

My new direction

⟹ A state without the means of some change is without the means
of its conservation. Edmund Burke

In this activity, we will bring together information you have built up about yourself in the earlier activities and put them into the context of the 'outside world' – external environment – so that you can set your course for your new direction.

A technique used widely in business to help in evaluating situations is SLOT analysis. SLOT stands for:

- Strengths
- Limitations
- Opportunities
- Threats

(SLOT is the American version. British people talk about SWOT analysis where 'W' stands for weakness – I'd rather talk about a person's limitations.)

The SLOT analysis can be an extremely useful technique for you to think about what you can offer, relative to your external environment, i.e. the job market. The SLOT analysis helps you to take stock of your position so that you can plan what you want to do next.

The strengths and limitations elements are personal to you. Opportunities and threats lie in the external environment.

Use the forms on the next pages to build up your own SLOT analysis. It will probably take a few days so do some work on it and keep coming back to it.

Use your SLOT analysis to:

- Identify how you can maximise the use of your strengths.
- See how you can compensate for your limitations.

● Identify opportunities, particularly ones which may not be immediately obvious.

● If at all possible see if threats can be turned into opportunities.

The first part of the exercise (strengths and limitations) will be straightforward, if you have completed the earlier activities. Opportunities and threats may be more difficult to identify so here are a few examples.

Opportunities: As society changes and technology advances new jobs emerge: 'conveyancing' shops no longer need a qualified solicitor. Computers need systems analysts/programmers/operators. The internet allows people to work in different locations, many even telecommute and do business with people at the other side of the word in split-seconds. New prisons are opening with 'contracted' staff. People are becoming more environmentally conscious. 'Fringe' medicine is becoming more acceptable. People are becoming more aware of their health and fitness. These are areas where new jobs are emerging.

Threats: These are the external barriers to you achieving your career goals. Like the closure of a major company in your area. Try to see if external threats can be turned into opportunities. It can sometimes be done. Diane, a friend of mine, wanted to return to her work as a teacher after starting a family. The external 'threat' to her doing it was that there was no suitable childcare available. If Diane and Keith, her husband, were having difficulty finding nursery places then surely other parents would be having the same problem? Their answer was to start a day-care nursery. Now, in addition to Diane's job as a teacher and Keith's as a college lecturer, they jointly run a nursery employing four people.

MY SLOT ANALYSIS

S My personal strengths	L My personal limitations

MY SLOT ANALYSIS

In my external environment	
O Opportunities	T Threats

EVALUATING YOUR SLOT ANALYSIS

Your SLOT analysis won't provide an instant and magic answer, but, in my experience, very often ideas seem to jump out of the pages when you look at all four factors side by side.

If you are having difficulty coming up with ideas, the next part of this activity will help you.

RESEARCH TIME – JOB IDEAS

Even if you have got internet access and you try to do this part of the activity anywhere other than in your local library, where you have access to directories, careers brochures and a hundred and one sources of valuable information, you won't even scratch the surface.

Take yourself off to the library

Take yourself off to the library and ask the librarian to advise on suitable references both in the 'industry and organisations' and the 'careers' sections. Alternatively, go to your local careers office – they aren't just for school leavers. They're incredibly helpful people and some will start to act as your research assistants if you explain what you are doing and ask for their advice in the right way! Many of them also have free access to the internet and will help you to find your way around if you ask. There are thousands of career sites, and I have listed some of them in an appendix but visit our career planning community at www.TheJobSearchersSuperstore.com for an up-to-date listing.

Don't be in too much of a hurry. Brainstorm ideas with your partner and friends.

Research isn't a 'do it' once and you're finished process either. Keep coming back to this section to add new ideas and to give you inspiration.

Use the tables on the next two pages to collect your thoughts.

JOB IDEAS 1

My ideal job will provide the following: Write into the boxes what you would like.

Uses for my skills and knowledge	Responsibilities
Working conditions and locality	Salary/benefits package
Interpersonal environment	Opportunities

JOB IDEAS 2

Places where I may be able to find my ideal job: Write down the names of companies, government bodies, charitable organisations, etc. where you may be able to find your ideal job – use library, friends, internet, networking contacts, and yourself as resources.

JOB IDEAS 3

Job names: Write down the names of jobs you could do.

DECISION-MAKING TIME!

When you have invested time and effort in the job ideas exercise, you will arrive at a vast number of options – especially when you combine the different jobs and the different potential workplaces.

If you had an army of secretaries and researchers working for you, then you could allocate tasks and blitz every possibility straight away. The reality of life is that you are probably on your own, so you need to set priorities so that you direct your energies in the right direction.

Now try to prioritise the options available to you so that you arrive at your top five priority targets. Your 'priority classification criteria' are the things on the job ideas 1 page (also see Activity 8). Very rarely will a job satisfy all of a person's 'ideal' criteria and the same person might identify their five top priority jobs as:

- An assistant brand manager in a large company.
- A market research executive in an agency.
- An advertising agency account executive.
- A market research manager in a large company.
- A brand manager in a small or medium-sized company.

The judge of the importance of each of your 'ideal' factors is you. Now write **your** five target positions below:

_____

_____

_____

_____

_____

Targeting

Having identified your priorities you still need to identify your top priority so that you can really target your jobsearch.

If you make your jobsearch too vague, then you will confuse people in your network, potential employers and recruitment consultants. Which of the above five options is your number one target, or is it difficult to choose?

People use many different decision-making methods. A technique which I have found useful is 'force-field analysis'. Quite simply, you write the pros and cons of making a decision alongside each other in lists. When you have collected all the pros and cons you allocate an arbitrary 'weighting', out of 10, to each point – only you can be the judge. Using force-field analysis takes only a few minutes and can really help in weighing the pros and cons of a decision.

Force-field analysis is a very useful, quick and simple way to evaluate the options available to you. It's a more structured way of weighing the pros and cons of a situation. Try it!

Active forces	Score	Restraining forces	Score
+ Positives Why should I go for this option?	Out of 10	– Negatives What's holding me back?	
Total +		Total –	

When you evaluate your five options using force-field analysis, the one with the highest score when you have subtracted the 'restraining forces' column from the 'active forces' column is the one you should go for as a first priority.

To give you an example: The force-field analysis on p. 84 is the one I used to help me to decide whether or not to start my own business.

FORCE-FIELD ANALYSIS EXAMPLE

Active forces + Positives Why should I go for this option?	Score	Restraining forces – Negatives What's holding me back?	
Master of my own destiny	10	Lack of predictable income	6
Earnings potential	7	Long-term security	5
Variety	7	Away from home?	5
Government aid/advice	5	Lack of permanence	3
Redundancy package available	8	Need office	2
I can set company's direction	8	Health insurance/life assurance	2
I am able to work alone	7	Pension	3
Market exists	7	Lack of challenge from peers	
Resources (me + support)	9	Collection of revenue	5
		Ability to obtain mortgage	5
		Not seeing job through	5
		No income	5
		No income	2
Total +	68	Total –	48

Even though there were **more negative reasons** than positive ones, the **'strength' of the positive argument won!**

PRIORITY 1 TARGET

Evaluate your options using the force-field analysis format below.

Aim for your number one target.

As you start to exhaust the possibilities for your number one target move to number two, etc.

Targeting your jobsearch gives you a clear direction to move in, just like having a well-printed map.

Active forces + Positives Why should I go for this option?	Score	Restraining forces – Negatives What's holding me back?	Score
Total +		Total –	

ACTIVITY (15)

Networking – contact development

➡ Putting off an easy thing makes it hard and putting off a hard one makes it impossible.   George H. Lonmer

A new word has entered the English language in the past few years: 'networking' or contact development. For many, it's something they have been doing for years quite naturally. For others the thought of it makes them feel so uncomfortable that it makes the hairs on the back of their neck stand up.

I talk about networking in Activity 28 'The way in – finding vacant jobs' and in other parts of the book. However, I believe that networking is so important to you in your jobsearch that it deserves a separate mention. Networking is the proactive process of maximising the relationships you already have and using these contacts to help you to identify work opportunities. Why is networking important? Some people believe that as few as 25 per cent of jobs are ever advertised. But someone must know about the rest! Also, career consultants will tell you that networking becomes increasingly important as you get older. About 50 per cent of people over 40 find a job through personal contacts.

Networking is not about pestering people for a job to the point that none of your friends will ever speak to you. Neither is it about embarrassing people so that they feel morally obliged to help you or even give you a job.

Networking is about approaching people genuinely to ask for advice and ideas on how you can get your next job: You aren't meeting them, telephoning or writing to them for a job. This is extremely important. When you make it quite clear that what you want from them is advice and ideas, you'll reduce their embarrassment about the contact and you will find them far more forthcoming.

On the practical front, just look at the power of numbers. Imagine you start off with the top 15 people in your network (see later), you contact these people and they each give you the names of two of their contacts. That's an extra 30 people and you now have a network of 45. You speak to each of them and get two more names. You now have a network of 105 people and you contact your 60 new contacts and get two more names, now you're up to 225 ... hang on, let's not get silly! There will be people who you can't contact for whatever reason, etc. I simply want to show that, using this process, it's not difficult to have 40 or 50 (or more!) people helping you in your jobsearch. People like to have their ego stroked by being asked for advice and I believe that most people will help if they are asked. You'll only embarrass them if it appears that you're asking them for a job.

Anyway, enough of their embarrassment! Broadcasting that you're on the dole (if you are) is a real ego booster for you isn't it?! I think not. So how are you going to say it? Some people find it very difficult to tell others that they are looking for work, so if we can overcome this barrier quickly you will be able to start networking straight away. Look at the following expressions.

Words used to describe what has happened to an organisation

Restructured	Gone bankrupt	We merged with another company
Contracted	Called in the receivers	We re-engineered
Downsized	The banks foreclosed	We had a change of management
Re-organised	We were taken over	We had a de-merger

Words used to describe the effects it has on people

Fired	Organised out	Dismissed	Booted out
Sacked	Let go	Axed	Dropped
Given P45	Said good-bye	Bounced	Let out
Made redundant	Surplus	Discharged	Terminated

In the space below write down why you are looking for work. Don't be self-effacing and don't be critical of your (previous) employer.

_____

_____

_____

_____

Now say it four or five times out loud.

The 'bottom line' is still the same, but you should now feel a lot more comfortable in explaining to people why you're looking for work and why you're asking for their help and advice.

WHO SHOULD I CONTACT?

Many people think they have only a small network of personal contacts until they do this exercise. Go through your address book, diary, business card file, customer records, correspondence files, etc. and brainstorm. Write down the names of people whom you know in the appropriate spaces on the next two pages.

Once completed, these two pages will be some of the most valuable pages in this book.

At this point **include anyone and everyone you can think of**. Ask your partner and close friends for ideas. **You have started networking!**

MY NETWORK

Bankers	Competitors
Customers	**Club members**
Consultants	**Doctors/dentist/solicitor**

Friends

MY NETWORK (continued)

Neighbours	Professional contacts
Suppliers	University/college/school colleagues
Past employers	Relatives
Teachers	Work colleagues

You can also develop 'virtual' contacts through internet chat rooms and forums (see Activity 29 E-jobsearching).

NOW I'VE GOT MY NETWORK – WHAT NEXT?

We need to identify whom you should contact first. So who are the best people to contact from your network?

- People whom you can contact relatively easily.
- Aim high – the higher up the organisation the better.
- People who could potentially employ you are even better.
- People on the same level, but different function who can 'pass you on' to their peer. (People on the same level with the same function may see you as a competitor.) People on a lower level are rarely useful except for information-gathering.

Now **choose the top 15 names** on your list and contact them. Decide which approach will be best. As a general principle: first choice is see them in person, second telephone, third is write a letter and the least favoured option is to send an E-mail. Remember, your objective is not simply to inform people of the fact that you're looking for work, you want to motivate them to do something to help you. The more personal your contact, the more likely it is to succeed. Of course there are exceptions. If you're working in the Netherlands and have a friend in Japan who may be able to help you to get a job in California then E-mail might work. But then again it might not! Don't get me wrong. I'm not a technophobe and I couldn't do my job as a consultant and author without E-mail. It's excellent for maintaining business contacts and exchanging information, but as a starting point for network development it's my least favourite option.

Whatever you do, get to the point quickly, don't waste their time. Achieve your three objectives:

1 To **let them know you are looking for work** – so that they can keep their eyes and ears open.

2 To **ask them for the names of two of their contacts** whom you might approach.

3 To **ask for their advice** about opportunities/recruitment consultants/ journals/ ads they might have seen.

Remember, you get one opportunity to make a first impression. The most powerful 'in' you can get is a personal introduction. As people give you the names of people in their network do what you can to make a positive first impression.

Don't over-stretch yourself by using the blunderbuss technique. If you try to contact everyone in your network on day one you won't be able to handle the workload. Keep prioritising and manage the project, e.g. following up with a phone call if you've said you will.

Whenever you have made contact with one of your network, either in person, or by telephone, send a short 'thank-you' letter, or an E-mail! It costs little and shows your genuine appreciation.

Happy networking!

'A goal is a dream taken seriously', or put another way – from 'South Pacific': 'You've got to have a dream, if you don't have a dream, how you going to have a dream come true?' In this activity we will formalise your dreams about the future into goals.

ACTIVITY (16)

Goal setting

➡ When I was young I observed that nine out of every ten things I did were failures,
so I did ten times more work.   George Bernard Shaw

WHY IS GOAL SETTING IMPORTANT?

Goal setting gives you a target to aim for. Organisations and businesses constantly use goal setting to help them to achieve things like production and sales targets. Similarly, many successful people say that an element of their success is due to goal setting. Goals are specific: 'to be happy' is not a goal. It is an aim. Achieving goals is the process of putting one foot after the next, along the stepping stones, which lead to happiness. A good test of a goal is to see if it is **SMART:**

Specific – e.g. if it is to get a job, list the title, type of organisation, etc.

Measurable – What criteria will you use to measure your achievement?

Achievable – You will become demotivated if you fail to achieve your goal – but don't make it too easy, make it challenging.

Relevant – Goals should directly relate to what you want to achieve.

Timed – Set a target completion date.

An example of a jobsearcher's goals could be:

'Each day next week I will make contact with a minimum of three people on my network list and will get two more names from each of them.'

A longer term goal might be:

'Within four months I will get a job as a development engineer, in a medium/large electronics company, within 30 miles of home, on £X000 per year.'

I know they sound a bit wordy but 'I'm going to make some phone calls and I'm going to get a job in electronics', just aren't goals. Goals state what you need to do to reach your aims.

Goals can be short or long term and relate to all aspects of life.

Use the form on the next page to help you to set your goals. Set the long-term goals first, then your short-term goals.

GOAL SETTING

I am going to achieve the following career and life goals in the next five years.

Goals	Home and family	Work	Social and community	Self (leisure, study, etc.)
Long term: 6 months				
1 year				
2 years				
5 years				
Short term: Today				
1 week				
1 month				

Make a note below of what you might need to do to resolve any conflicts:

_____

_____

_____

_____

ACTIVITY ⟨17⟩

Managing my jobsearching project

> ⇒ Lost yesterday, somewhere between sunrise and sunset, two golden hours, each set with sixty diamond minutes. No reward is offered, they are gone forever.   Horace Mann

If you're currently working and also jobsearching then you have a challenging job balancing your time between the two. If your current full-time occupation is jobsearching then the apparent lack of structure can be daunting. It can scare some people into doing anything; that bit of decorating I've been putting off, or a visit to long lost friends – anything other than jobsearching. The answer to both is to have planning and control systems.

ORGANISE YOURSELF AND MANAGE YOUR TIME

Jobsearching is a job.

- Allocate some 'office space' at home where you can work undisturbed. If you haven't got one, buy, beg or borrow a PC with a good printer. Don't be put off by thinking that you have to have the latest 'all singing and dancing' PC. You'll need something decent if you're surfing the Net for jobs, but for word-processing you can pick up a bargain from the newspaper.

- Keep a diary and use it both for planning your time and recording appointments.

- In addition to the files on your hard disk, have a paper-based 'filing system', either using files, box files or ring binders.

- Work expands to fill the time available – set deadlines for each task.

- Set daily objectives; use the daily action planner on page 99 and stick to it.

- Prioritise the day's tasks: A: must; B: should; C: could. Only move to the Bs when the As are finished, and to the Cs when the Bs are finished. Don't do the Cs first just because they can be done quickly. Subdivide As into A1, A2, A3, and **do A1 now!**

- Block off times in your diary for different parts of your jobsearch.
- Decide when you are at your best for doing things, e.g. best at telephoning early morning, good at planning early evening.
- Plan for tomorrow at the end of today.
- Start each day by making progress against an A1.
- After you have opened and sorted your mail, handle each piece of paper only once – in other words, only pick up a piece of paper from your 'in' tray when you intend to do something with it.
- Accumulate non-essential reading together and scan it for 20 minutes each week.
- Add additional actions to your personal action plan as they arise throughout the day and prioritise them.
- Each week complete the weekly jobsearch report (see below), as an evaluation of how you are progressing against achieving your goals.

PROCRASTINATION IS THE THIEF OF TIME. DO IT NOW!

Don't be like a colleague of my friend Ann, who bought a motivational cassette tape on procrastination, but never got round to listening to it!

JOBSEARCH PERFORMANCE AND PLANNING SUMMARY

Week ending (day/date:)

THIS WEEK	GOALS FOR NEXT WEEK
I wrote _____ jobsearch letters I sent ____ résumés and ____letters to potential employers I completed _____ applications I made _____ jobsearch telephone calls I completed _____ hours of job research I set up _____ appointments for network interviews I conducted _____ networking interviews I received _____ invitations to a job interview I followed up on __ contacts and____ referrals	I will complete _____ applications I will make _____ jobsearch telphone calls I will complete _____ hours of job research I will set up _____ appointments for networking interviews I will conduct ____ networking interviews I will follow up on _____contacts and ___ referrals

(*Copyright waiver:* This form may be photocopied for personal use of purchasers.)

PERSONAL ACTION PLAN

Your name:		Date:		
Today's goals:				
Action plan:		A/B/C	Deadline	Completed

Carry forward uncompleted tasks to tomorrow:

(Copyright waiver: This form may be photocopied for personal use of purchasers.)

ACTIVITY 18

Working for myself

➡ Diligence is the mother of good luck.   Benjamin Franklin

> HEALTH AND WEALTH WARNING
>
> ## DON'T DO IT!

Have I put you off? The chances are that your earnings will be lower than you anticipate. Your working hours will be longer than you have ever worked before and you will stretch your personal relationships to their limits, or maybe even beyond.

It may be that as you have worked through the activities in this book you have started to think that you would like to become self-employed. If my health and wealth warning was all that was needed to put you off then I've done you a great favour! You'll appreciate the scope of this book is to advise people on how to gain paid employment.

If you're considering self-employment gather as much information as you can. The Department of Employment has an excellent 'Induction scheme' (details from your job centre) for new business start-ups. The high street banks produce free information packs (the NatWest one is very useful). Contact your local tec/business link.

Talk to as many people as you can who run their own businesses: your friendly fish and chip shop owner; local landlord, newsagent, etc. No matter what the business, the potential problems are usually the same – cash flow, marketing, obtaining supplies. With the greatest of respect to college lecturers and counsellors, it will only be from talking to self-employed people that you'll find out what it's really like. You'll also hear, no doubt, of the enormous satisfaction that comes from being self-employed. But I don't want to over-sell.

Research, research, research – and be wary of others. Partnerships even among 'best friends' often collapse because of disagreements. The figures show that the majority of new businesses fail. You may be able to reduce the risk by buying a franchise, but even franchises fail. I know from bitter experience of having personally lost over £30,000 in cash, and as much again in other ways, on a franchise. I was lied to when the person sold me the franchise. But I could have avoided my losses and walked away from the 'opportunity' if I had researched the company more thoroughly. I should have talked to many, many more people. Learn from my mistake. Ask to see audited accounts, ask to speak to suppliers, ask to see actual sales figures and profits, ask to speak to satisfied customers, ask the person who's selling you the franchise to produce factual evidence of their previous successes. If anything doesn't look right, then walk away. There are plenty more fish in the sea. The financial and psychological scars from my experience will take many years to heal.

Most important of all, talk your idea through with your partner (if you have one). His/her support is essential.

If, when you have gathered all of the information, you are totally committed to it, abandon your jobsearch. You cannot do either of them half-heartedly and ... Go for it!

Good luck. You'll need it.

(Website addresses where you can get further information at www.TheJobSearchersSuperstore.com.)

ACTIVITY 19

Interim management, freelancing and consulting

➡ There will never be a system invented which will do away with the
necessity for work.   Henry Ford

For many people, interim management, freelancing, consulting or becoming part
of the 'talent market' gives freedom from having a 'real job' without the risk of
setting off in a completely different direction and starting a new business.

OUTSOURCING – A NEW WORK PARADIGM

Years ago, 'consultant' was a word that many executives put on their CV to cover
a period of unemployment. The world is now very different. Many organisations
have taken the decision to concentrate on their 'core' business and to 'outsource'
or buy in expertise as needed. Improvements in employee rights and the rising
cost of making staff redundant also mean that companies are very wary of
increasing headcount if they can avoid it. This creates a phenomenal number of
opportunities for people who can be contracted in for short periods. Some people,
especially in skill-shortage areas, keep busy through temporary work and interim
management assignments, gained through employment agencies. If this kind of
lifestyle appeals to you then start contacting recruitment agencies that specialise
in 'temp' and 'interim assignments' and build a relationship with a small selected
number.

I could write a whole book on the dos and dont's of consulting (now there's an
idea!). If you're considering going it alone as a freelancer, or consultant here's a
starting point.

STARTING OUT AS A FREELANCER/CONSULTANT: 4 KEYS TO SUCCESS

1 Your vision of what success means to you. What are you hoping to achieve for yourself?

2 Your skill and knowledge set. What have you got that people will want to buy in? How will you add value to your customer's organisation?

3 Maximise profitability by generating revenue. Communication: marketing and selling. How will people learn who you are and then make the decision to use you?

4 Maximise profitability by controlling costs. Budgeting and cash flow control.

ACTION PLAN

Don't talk to potential customers … until you have done all of the following:

- Established your vision of what success means to you. It took me nearly a month when I first started out.

- Convinced yourself that you've got something to offer. If you can't convince yourself, then how will you convince a customer?

- Clarified what you're offering. When I first started out I made the mistake of trying to offer too much. Potential customers were confused. When I focused on one area of expertise, training and development, business took off.

- Established that the market exists. Do your market research (OK, you'll need to talk to potential customers to do this, but remember, you're in asking mode).

- Prepared a business plan and a marketing plan.

- Prepared a budget and a cash flow forecast (guidelines and even free software are available from your friendly bank manager).

- Decided what you're going to charge. Which sector of the market? Aldi, Lidl, Kwik-Save, Asda/Wal-Mart, Tesco, Marks & Spencer, Waitrose and Fortnum and Mason all sell groceries, but their products and prices are targeted at different market sectors.

- Picked your professional advisers. My bookkeeper and my accountant are both freelancers and have been with me for almost a decade.

- Chosen a name for your business and got an URL (website address). You may find it easier to check what website names are available, and then choose your trading name. (Link at www.TheJobSearchersSuperstore.com)

- Established how you're going your finance the start-up. Even if you can do it on a shoe-string and you can win some business in your first week, it may be weeks or even months, before the cheques start to roll in.

- Set up your office: I know hot-desking (last one into the office gets the cleaners cupboard) and 'virtual offices' (have laptop and mobile phone, will consult) are becoming popular, but I'm a bit old-fashioned and I like to have my own office space.

- Talked to your tax office.

- Talked to a financial planning advisor about insurance, such as office contents and vehicle, pensions and professional liability.

- Got free advice on start-ups from your local TEC/Business Link.

- Set up customer records and systems like credit and invoicing procedures. Establish your trading terms and conditions and drawn up model contracts. All pretty boring stuff, but essential if you are going to be taken seriously. Fortunately there's lots of good, inexpensive software around to guide you through the maze.

By all means produce a nice logo and some product literature, but I can't emphasise too much the importance of networking when working as a 'freelancer'. I started working as a consultant in 1990. Since then, I'd say that 90 per cent of the work that I have got has been through personal contacts (better re-read the section on networking!).

(Website addresses where you can get further information in Appendix 1 and at www.TheJobSearchersSuperstore.com.)

HOW WILL I GET THERE?

The tactics of how to get the

job you want

INTRODUCTION TO STEP 3

The three great essentials to achieve anything worthwhile are first, hard work; second, stick-to-itiveness; third, common sense.

Thomas A. Eddison

What we have done so far has been to develop your strategic direction. This section is devoted to the tactics of getting a job.

Think of each of the activities as a different skill of a craftsperson – you. The activities are the tools to help you to get your new job.

Work on those activities which will help you to develop those skills which you need to help you to get the job you want.

ACTIVITY 20

Using the telephone to my advantage

⇒ Speak clearly, if you speak at all;
carve every word before you let it fall.

Oliver Wendell Holmes

Used effectively the telephone can get you past security guards, along hallowed corridors and into the office of decision-makers!

Whether you are telephoning to confirm an appointment for an interview or at the start of your jobsearch, you will find the following tips, which are taught to telesales people, helpful:

- Make sure you have a pen and paper ready along with any relevant documents.

- Smile – I know it feels silly when you're the only one in the room, but it adds sparkle to your voice.

- Stand up! All your internal viscera are pushing up against your diaphragm and squeezing the confidence out of your voice. Standing up makes you more assertive and makes you sound more convincing!

- Have a clear objective of what you want to achieve, along with a fall-back, e.g. primary objective to arrange an informal meeting; secondary objective to call back tomorrow, when they have had a chance to read your résumé, to arrange a meeting.

- Make sure your language is convincing, fluent and understandable.

- Prepare your script in advance – write down your agenda.

- Practise your script, e.g. the direct approach:

    'Hello Mr _____. Ms _____. I'm _____. You recently received a copy of my résumé. I'm calling to see if we can make an appointment to meet informally to discuss any vacancies you might have for management accountants?'

- Have your diary ready!

- Keep a written record of every conversation.

OVERCOMING DEFENCES

The higher up the organisation you go, the higher and wider the barriers seem to become with receptionists and secretaries seemingly having no other purpose than to protect their bosses!

The higher up the organisation you go ...

The following techniques range from the polite to the devious. All of them work!

- Find out the secretary's name from the receptionist. Address him/her personally and repeat the name at least twice when requesting to be put through.

- When you're networking and you're put through to a secretary say it's 'a personal call' (most managers will take 'personal calls' since most of them think it's a call from a head-hunter!). Get to the point quickly. If it's a friend of a friend, make sure you clarify it straight away.

- Beat the system by calling the manager at around 8.00 am or after 6.00 pm (i.e. before or after work for most secretaries) or when the secretary is at lunch.

- If you try phoning most companies during normal working hours and ask for the name of the marketing director, almost invariably the receptionists will tell you politely, but firmly, that they are not allowed to give that information over the telephone.

  Ring at around 8.30 pm and you're likely to speak to a lonely security guard, who is looking after the telephones, along with the odd million pounds' worth of building! Speak to them politely and explain that you want to call the marketing director the next day and you just wanted to make sure you'd got the right offices. They'll be glad of someone to talk to and will probably reel off a list of names and extension numbers – if you ask for them, have your pen ready.

- Use a 'third-party recommendation' like 'Mr Robinson, your personnel manager has asked me to get in touch with …'

Remember, you may need to kiss a lot of frogs before you can find a prince! But persistence does pay!

ACTIVITY 21

Letter writing and E-mail

⇒ A law of nature rules that energy cannot be destroyed. You change its form from coal to steam, from steam to power in the turbine, but you do not destroy energy. In the same way, another law governs human activity and rules that honest effort cannot be lost, but that some day the proper benefits will be forthcoming.   Paul Speicher

If you can see someone in person do it. If you can't see them personally, speak to them on the telephone. If you can't speak to them on the telephone, write a letter. If they are on the other side of the world or you can only get their E-mail address, or you need a quick reply, send an E-mail. Both traditional 'snail-mail' and E-mail have their uses and, realistically, you will have to write a lot of letters and send a lot of E-mails. Learn from the people in direct marketing who write letters to customers for a living. Why? Because through your letters you are trying to sell another person the idea that 'they should meet you', that 'they should look at your CV', etc. When it comes down to it, it's a sales letter.

AIDA is the copywriter's greatest friend. If you look at well-written 'direct mail' letters they follow the AIDA format:

A   Attention – The first paragraph quickly comes to the point to grab the reader's attention.

I   Interest – The second gives information to arouse the reader's interest.

D   Desire – The third paragraph talks about the benefits you will gain and what it will be like for you to own the product or service.

A   Action – Now you want the product or service what do you do? Telephone, fill a form etc.?

Sounds simple doesn't it? Would that it were that straightforward!

As you write letters of application, letters to networking contacts, letters to request application forms, covering letters to go with your CV, or letters to recruitment consultants and E-mails, check to see if they follow the AIDA principles.

Try to see the letter or E-mail from the recipient's viewpoint. What impression would it make on you? What would you do when you received it?

The following pages contain some general tips on letter writing which many people who are unused to letter writing find useful. After the 'model letters' are some tips on using E-mail.

LETTER WRITING – USEFUL TIPS

- Use quality paper. A4, ideally. If you want to push the boat out get some stationery printed at your high street print-shop. (Don't ask for the address to be printed in blue – it doesn't photocopy too well.)

- Handwriting is OK if it's legible. A word-processed letter is almost always OK, unless you have been specifically asked to submit a hand-written application. If you're using an ink-jet printer, make sure it's set to the best print quality.

- There should be no spelling mistakes, grammatical errors or scruffy layout. But that can't happen! Don't you believe it! When I recruited a secretary recently I rejected over half of the applications for these reasons. The advertisement asked for 'accuracy'! Fortunately, modern software packages check as you type. If it's an older package make sure you run the spell-check and the grammar check.

- Write to a named person whenever you can.

- 'Dear Mr' is straightforward for men. If you don't know whether a woman is a 'Mrs' or 'Miss' then 'Ms' is the safest bet these days. These letters end 'Yours sincerely' (small 's').

- When you have to write 'Dear Sir' or 'Dear Madam' (note, no 'e' at the end), then these letters end 'Yours faithfully' (small 'f').

- If an advertisement asks you to apply to Peter Butler do not start letter 'Dear Peter' – it's over-familiar unless you know Peter personally. Even then be cautious, since your letter may be photocopied and circulated to other people.

- Be succinct – get to the point quickly. If your letter is more than one page long, then edit it to fit on one page.

- Match the skills and knowledge that you have to the ones the recruiter is looking for, i.e. those mentioned either in the job description or the advertisement.

● Never, never, never be self-effacing – 'I'm not quite what you're looking for but I'll give it a go anyway!' And don't point out anything which is missing from your portfolio of skills and knowledge that they are looking for! It's their job to spot that!

On the following pages I have included some sample letters. They are not offered as definitive examples, but hopefully they will provide the spark of inspiration you need if you are sitting staring out of the window with a blank sheet of paper in front of you!

WARNING! One of the wonderful things about modern word-processing packages is that you can do mail merges, cut and paste information and copy files all with the click of a mouse and a few keystrokes. Check that the name at the start of the address matches the salutation (the Dear Mr or Ms bit). If you haven't got an eye for detail ask someone who has to proofread and check for you. Letters addressed to Colonel Mustard that start 'Dear Professor Plum' go straight into the bin! And take my word for it, it does happen.

Letter to request an application form

4 Stable Cottages
Abthorpe
Northamptonshire
NN12 8QT
Tel 123 7777777

23 March 2001

Mr G Choice
Moderate Corporation
Science Park
Daventry Road
Northants
NN99 99NN

Dear Mr Choice

RE: CE/23393

I noticed your advertisement in the *Chronicle & Echo* newspaper for a laboratory supervisor. I would be very grateful if you will send me an application form.

I look forward to hearing from you.

Yours sincerely

Janet Dickson (Mrs)

NOTE

● Don't enclose a CV or anything else at this point. Follow their system.

Covering letter with CV

4 Stable Cottages
Abthorpe
Northamptonshire
NN12 8QT
Tel 123 7777777

23 March 2001

Mr G Choice
Moderate Corporation
Science Park
Daventry Road
Northants
NN99 99NN

Dear Mr Choice

I would like to apply for the post of accounts supervisor which was advertised recently in the *Chronicle & Echo*.

I have read the job description with great interest and enclose my completed application form.

I look forward to hearing from you.

Yours sincerely

Janet Dickson (Mrs)

NOTE

- Don't antagonise them by implying that you're bound to get an interview. If you are too presumptuous you'll turn them off.
- This letter does very little, however, to help the recruiter to match the candidate to the job. It would have been a good idea to include three or four feature, advantage or benefit statements (see Activity 24 'Selling myself').

Response to an advertised vacancy

4 Stable Cottages
Abthorpe
Northamptonshire
NN12 8QT
Tel 123 7777777

23 March 2001

Mr G Choice
Moderate Corporation
Science Park
Daventry Road
Northants
NN99 99NN

Dear Mr Choice

Ref: MCC/737 – Production manager: *Chronicle & Echo,* **22nd May 2001**

I am writing in response to the above advertisement and wish to apply for the position.

You will see from my CV that, for the past five years, I have managed a plant manufacturing shampoos and hair colourants on a continuous production basis. Many of the production features appear to be very similar to your own. Previously I worked as Materials Planning Manager in a high-volume batch production plant.

I believe I have all of the qualities you have outlined in your advertisement – BS5750 trained, a strong leader and capacity for hard work.

I am now seeking an appointment where my experience can be fully utilised.

I look forward to hearing from you.

Yours sincerely

Janet Dickson (Mrs)

NOTE

● This letter highlights what the candidate has to offer against the recruiter's requirements, but isn't a 're-write' of the CV.

A speculative letter to a targeted potential employer

4 Stable Cottages
Abthorpe
Northamptonshire
NN12 8QT
Tel 123 7777777

23 March 2001

Mr G Choice
Moderate Corporation
Science Park
Daventry Road
Northants
NN99 99NN

Dear Mr Choice

Ref: An Opportunity to Increase Your Market Share and Reduce Operating Costs

As the Marketing Director (Electronic Products) of a £50m turnover UK company, I have initiated and managed improvement programmes that have reversed sales and profit declines.

Some of my achievements include:
- launching 6 new products over the last two years and increasing market share substantially.
- increasing sales by 12% by exploiting new markets.
- reducing marketing operation overheads by £125,000 by introducing effective controls.
- introducing networked computer-based information and financial control systems to improve customer response times and invoicing.
- sales and profit forecasting on a monthly basis with 90% + accuracy.

My CV is enclosed as I am now actively looking for a new position. I would be very glad to give you more information or to come and see you.

Yours sincerely

Janet Dickson (Mrs)

Enc.

NOTE

● Four or five achievement statements should be just right. You want to stimulate their interest and leave them wanting to know more.

Making something out of nothing

4 Stable Cottages
Abthorpe
Northamptonshire
NN12 8QT
Tel 123 7777777

23 March 2001

Mr G Choice
Moderate Corporation
Science Park
Daventry Road
Northants
NN99 99NN

Dear Mr Choice

It was kind of you to read my CV and write to me on 19th March.

I was disappointed to learn that there are no openings in your company. It would have been a fortunate coincidence if my letter had reached you when you were recruiting for someone with my background.

May I ask you whether you can suggest the names of any other people whom I might contact?

I know that managers like yourself are often asked by others to 'keep their eyes open' for people with my skills and knowledge. I would very much appreciate you referring me to any of your acquaintances who could be interested. I shall welcome any additional suggestions that you can give.

Many thanks in anticipation.

Yours sincerely

Janet Dickson (Mrs)

NOTE

● What have you got to lose? This letter is also worth trying with recruitment consultants – they may refer you to a 'competitor'.

Speculative letter to a recruitment consultant

4 Stable Cottages
Abthorpe
Northamptonshire
NN12 8QT
Tel 123 7777777

23 March 2001

Ms H Hunter
Choose Well Consultants
Northampton Road
Wappenham
Northants
NN99 9NN

Dear Ms Hunter

I am seeking a new appointment where my general management experience in the hotel and catering industry can be used. Any dynamic and developing business area which involves direct customer contact would particularly interest me. I am also keen to continue to develop my general management skills.

My present company is undergoing a period of substantial change and so I believe this an ideal opportunity to review my career to date and investigate other possibilities.

I am willing to relocate within Europe. My current remuneration package includes: a basic salary of £29,000 per annum, a 10% (variable) bonus, fully expensed car, private healthcare and a non-contributory pension scheme.

I enclose my CV and will be glad of any advice you can provide.

Yours sincerely

Janet Dickson (Mrs)

NOTE

- Note that salary package details are included in approaches to recruitment consultants so that they can match you against vacancies. Also, different consultants often deal with jobs at different levels.

Follow-up thank-you letter after networking

4 Stable Cottages
Abthorpe
Northamptonshire
NN12 8QT
Tel 123 7777777

23 March 2001

Mr G Choice
Moderate Corporation
Science Park
Daventry Road
Northants
NN99 99NN

Dear Mr Choice

Many thanks for meeting with me last week. I really did appreciate the comments you made about the way I have embarked on my jobsearch.

Thank you also for putting me in contact with Simon and Pat. I have arranged to meet Pat next week, but Simon seems to spend all of his time in meetings – I'll keep trying!

I'll let you know how I get on.

Kind regards.

Yours sincerely

Janet Dickinson

NOTE

- This letter is far less formal than any of the others, but is still businessike.
- If you promise a friend that you'll let them know how you got on, then do it – they want to know and in a couple of weeks they may have some new information for you!

E-MAIL – USEFUL TIPS

I'm sitting in my office in rural Lincolnshire and have been catching up on some of my mail. I have just dropped notes on the desks of a client in San Francisco, a friend in Los Angeles, a friend who lives three miles away and sent a proposal to a client in London. The whole job took less time than it takes to go to the post box! The wonders of E-mail! I think I heard somewhere that it travels at 3,000 miles per second!

The use of E-mail has revolutionised the way many people work, and varies from being the bane of people's lives, to their most important working tool. I spoke to a number of recruiters when researching this section and was told that about 50 per cent of applications arrive by E-mail nowadays and it's rising.

The speed of information exchange can be phenomenal. You can see a job advertised in the morning's newspaper, E-mail for information and have submitted your E-mail application, with completed application form and attached CV, before you have had your second cup of coffee of the day!

Correct use of E-mails can augment the effectiveness of your jobsearch, so here are a few dos and dont's.

Do:

- Understand the difference between urgent and important. It's important that you contact people in the right way. Because you're communicating electronically don't pressurise yourself into rushing and making mistakes.

- Keep your message short. Aim to fill no more than one screen. I prefer to use a very short E-mail message, with a 'proper' letter, along with a CV as separate attachments. Others prefer the letter of application in the body of the E-mail.

- Put your telephone number and address at the end of your E-mail.

- Print-off any attachments before sending to ensure that they are correctly formatted.

- Check that the recipient can read your files if you are sending letters or CV attachments. It would appear that MS Word has become the 'standard' and I haven't yet had an occasion when someone couldn't read my MS Word files, but if you're using an unusual word processor, it's worth sending a quick message to say that you would like to apply for the job and attach a CV, what format should be used for attachments? In a similar way some companies block E-mails from free service providers, such as Hotmail, as a way of cutting down junk mail – check.

- Ask yourself: What do you want the recipient to know and do when they have read your message?
- Use an attention-grabbing subject line.
- Use short sentences (35 words max).
- Use your spell and grammar checker (my word processor tells me if I have made a mistake, but my E-mail package doesn't).
- Reply quickly.
- Ask someone else to proofread and check your application.

Don't:

- 'Blast-mail'. I know it's easier and cheaper to write one message and then group-send it to 20 or 30 recruiters, but put yourself in the recruiter's shoes. Which approach do you prefer, a personal approach or the blunderbuss?
- Write E-mails on-line.
- Use heavy shading or fancy formatting, or complicated graphics and photographs. Your message won't photocopy well and some companies use special filters to block large files and pictures, so that their information highways don't become congested.
- Send password-protected documents as attachments. Yes, it does happen. Someone password protects their CV on their PC at work, so that colleagues can't read it. Then they see a job in the newspaper … Put yourself in the recruiter's shoes. You have had 60 applications for the same job are you really going to take the trouble to contact your mysterious candidate? Copy the information and paste into a new file, print to check that it retains its formatting. Send the new file as an attachment and then delete!
- Use smileys and emoticons.
- Delete your message once you have sent it.

- Be over-familiar; remember this is a business contact, not a bit of banter with an old school mate.

- Keep re-sending messages in a two-way conversation. Delete all but the most recent message.

Speculative applications and approaches by E-mail

The same rules apply here as approaching someone using a conventional letter, remember the AIDA formula.

There are many ways to find out someone's E-mail address, such as telephoning a receptionist or sending a message to their company's postmaster, e.g. postmaster@TheJobSearchersSuperstore.com. Most company websites contain E-mail addresses, but these are often only general enquiries addresses. If you want to target your approach you may have to do some digging. There are a number of internet directory sites, such as www.whowhere.com and many search engines such as Yahoo! and Netscape which provide access to E-mail directories. Not surprisingly the majority of sites cater for the USA, but the UK's catching up. One thing to bear in mind is that you might just find someone's personal or family E-mail address, and you might do more harm than good by sending an E-mail to them at home, rather than work. Also, you'll need to be sure that you're sending your E-mail to the right Jane Doe!

ACTIVITY 22

Writing my CV

➡ When I see a bird that walks like a duck and swims like a duck, I call that bird a duck. Richard Cardinal Cushing

Imagine yourself in your smartest clothes, looking as well-groomed as you have ever looked in your life and carrying that facial expression of quiet (but not arrogant) confidence.

Your CV (curriculum vitae), or résumé, or, as some call it, 'personal and career history', is a written equivalent to the mental picture you have just formed.

In almost all the contacts you make, whether networking, speculative applications or responses to advertisements, your CV and introductory letter will make the difference to whether or not you get an interview.

The decision between a 'regret' (sorry you've missed your chance), a 'regret, but hold' (you're not exactly what we're looking for at present but we'll keep your details on file) and an 'invite for interview' can be made in as little as 30 seconds!

If you think this is unrealistic then pity Geoff, a colleague of mine, who advertised two jobs in a car assembly plant and got 1400 replies! Or Beth, another friend, who is a personnel manager. She was so overwhelmed with responses to an advertisement for a secretary that all applications in brown envelopes or applications with second-class stamps were rejected. Two hundred responses to an advertisement is not at all uncommon. With applications on-line it can be even worse, and you may find yourself competing with people from all parts of the globe. You see recruitment is a selection process! What the recruiter is doing is filtering out all of the people who don't match their selection criteria. I understand that some on-line applications are even scanned by software to find word-matches. If the software doesn't find the criteria the recruiter is looking for the software generates an automatic 'thank-you but no thank-you' E-mail.

You need to help the recruiter positively to 'screen you in'. The job of your CV is to take you through the paper 'screening process' to an inteview. We'll look at on-line applications in Activity 29.

RECRUITERS ARE ALL DIFFERENT

There is an expression that goes: 'If you are ill and ask three Harley Street specialists for a second opinion then you'll get five different opinions!' In the same way recruiters have personal preferences in how they like to see CVs written. For these reasons it is not advisable to be dogmatic. Added to which, your CV is a very personal document – in the final analysis you are the best judge of whether your CV best represents you.

On page 130 is a 'CV summary' which will help you to gather the relevant information and some example CVs that will help you to decide on which layout you like best can be found on pages 133–143.

BASIC PRINCIPLES

- Use clean laser-printed originals, with a legible font, and stick to one font:

  This is in 8 point Times New Roman PS.

  `This is in 10 point New Courier.`

  ### This is in 12 point Helvetica.

- Use quality paper.

- Be brief – use one or two pages if possible. You can do it! Screening of CVs is brief. If the most relevant item is on page 7 paragraph 6, forget it!

- Beware of jargon! Write in plain English if you're a logistics manager, a military officer, a research scientist, etc. Indeed, if you are a specialist of any kind, you will almost certainly have your own vocabulary. Use plain English!

- Be specific – 'I have five years' experience in …' says far more than 'I have wide experience of …', as does 'I reduced inventory from £4.2m to £1.8m in a period of 12 months' compared with 'We made substantial savings by reducing our inventory'.

- Even if you can produce a decent letter it may be worth investing in getting someone to do your CV for you. Local newspapers and newsagents' windows are a good source. Ask to see previous examples and make sure they keep a copy for future updating and so that you can 'personalise' key strengths to produce a targeted CV to fit each job. Some of the modern software packages even have CV templates, but before you decide to use a template, make sure that you're comfortable with the style, layout and content. It's your CV.

- Proofread, proofread, proofread. Start at the bottom of the page and read backwards. You may thimk there are no mistakes, but by reading backwards you see each word in isolation and can spot errors and mis-spellings. For example, did you spot think in the last sentence or did you read what you thought was there?

- If you have a name which may be interpreted as male or female, such as Jay or Frankie, enter m or f in brackets. I'm certainly not advocating sexual discrimination in recruitment, but it puts recruiters off-balance when they phone candidates and get their sex wrong! If you think your name might cause confusion, you can also help recruiters if you explain. Name: Malcolm (given) Hornby (family). And if you were named Rebecca at birth and have since then been known only as Becky, then put Becky on your CV. Remember it's YOUR marketing tool.

- Some recruiters like a margin on the left-hand side so that they can make notes.

- CVs are often separated from letters of application. Ensure that your name and address are there clearly and write your name at the top of each page. It will help if pages become detached and it will also help an interviewer to remember your name when they are halfway through an interview!

- Presentation 'gimmicks' – personally I like to receive CVs from people who have had them bound or who have attached a photograph. It says that they are prepared to put that bit of extra effort into their application. I know, however, that many of my fellow human resources professionals would strongly disagree. Your decision has to be based on the job and what you know about the organisation.

- If you're applying for your first job or are returning to work after bringing up a family, help the recruiter to recognise your transferable skills. President of the outdoor pursuits society and qualified mountain leader implies leadership and someone trained to cope with adversity. Treasurer of the parish church council implies financial skills and abilities to deal with contractors, etc.; spell it out for them.

THE LANGUAGE OF CVS

'It ain't what you say, it's the way that you say it.' This is not totally true, but there is an element of truth to it! Striking a balance between being positive and sounding arrogant can be a real challenge.

Use active words not passive words: 'I was responsible for managing a project team which installed a new intranet' says more than 'I was involved in installing a new intranet'. The first statement is far more powerful, while the second statement might mean no more than you plugged it in and switched it on!

Passive words that you should avoid are: liaised with, co-ordinated and administered. The following action verbs will be useful for helping you to write your CV and for letters of application.

ACTION VERBS

accelerated	extended	reduced	terminated
accomplished	finished	reorganised	traced
achieved	generated	revised	traded
approved	implemented	scheduled	trained
conceived	improved	serviced	transferred
conducted	increased	simplified	translated
completed	introduced	set up	trimmed
consolidated	launched	sold	tripled
created	maintained	solved	turned
decided	negotiated	started	uncovered
delivered	ordered	structured	united
demonstrated	performed	streamlined	utilised
designed	pioneered	strengthened	vacated
developed	planned	stressed	waged
directed	processed	stretched	widened
doubled	programmed	succeeded	won
eliminated	promoted	summarised	worked
ended	proposed	superseded	wrote
established	purchased	supervised	
expanded	redesigned		

But beware; don't overdo it. The recruiter is looking for a mortal!

Try reading your finished version to your partner or close friend. If you go a little pink you're probably spot on – bright red and you've overdone it!

How to avoid the convoluted and imprecise expressions and words used by applicants – 'Brevity is best'.

AVOID	USE
As a result of this project the company's costs were cut by …	This cut costs by …
During the period referred to in the previous sentence …	I …
As a consequence of the success of this project I was asked to take up the more senior appointment of …	I was promoted …
In this position I …	I …
Considerable elements of my responsibilities were …	I was responsible for …
anticipate	expect
behind schedule	late
prior to	before
personnel	people
proceeded to	then
inaugurated	set up
initiated	started
terminated	ended

CV CHECKLIST

This checklist combines the should (in bold) and could (in italic) be included items. Use this in combination with the CV summary on the following pages to help you to gather information and to develop your own CV.

- Name, address and telephone number(s) stating daytime contact.

- *Marital status (some people prefer to exclude this).*

- *Number of dependants and ages (some people prefer to exclude this).*

- *Nationality.*

- *Date of birth/age.*

- School, college/university attended normally only from age of 11 onwards.

- Qualifications: for a recent graduate looking for a first job state GCSEs; level, subjects and pass grade, along with subjects taken and class of degree. For a 45-year-old divisional director, 6 'O' Levels, 3 'A' Levels, BSc 2(i) Chemistry is usually sufficient, although for some professions, e.g. accountancy, you may still wish to include GCSE 'A' Level grades.

- *Language proficiency.*

- *Willingness to relocate, especially if you're out of commuting distance (omit if you aren't).*

- Current/last job first, then work backwards through your career, allocating most space to recent job(s) with brief mentions of your early career. Give a one- or two-sentence summary of the company products/services and their annual turnover, summarise your responsibilities and achievements against each job.

- *Current/last salary and benefits package, e.g. company car. Be brief. (Opinions differ on whether salary should be included – you may wish to keep your cards close to your chest and risk missing an opportunity because they think you'll be 'too expensive'.)*

- *Career aims.*

- *Personal strengths.*

- *Leisure activities. Be realistic; a one-week skiing holiday five years ago does not qualify you as a skier! Include a variety to show that you have broad interests, but not too many – they may think you'll have no time left for work! Three to four activities are adequate.*

- *Professional achievements, e.g. titles of research papers or articles you have had published. But don't, like someone who once sent me a 27-page CV, attach the papers!*

- Memberships of professional institutions and whether by examination or election.
- Do not include referees, unless you're applying for a job in the public sector.
- Driving licence – clean and current don't mean the same!

You need to help the reader positively to 'screen you in'

CV SUMMARY

Name:	Address:	Tel:

Strengths: *A four or five **short** sentences of **your** personal strengths. A four- or five-sentence summary of your career; who you are and what you have to offer. Make every word count!*

Education and qualifications: *Right here up front if you have a first class honours degree, PhD and MBA. You may wish to leave to the end if your business achievements outshine your academic ones!*

Career history: *Most recent first and work backwards. Include responsibilities and quantified achievements. Reduce the information as you go back, e.g., five achievements for your current/most recent job. One from a job 15 years ago.*

Professional memberships etc:

Personal information: Willingness to relocate, marital status, etc.

'READYMADE' TEMPLATES

Many of today's word-processing packages contain excellent pre-formatted CV templates. There are also lots of ideas to be had from the jobsites on the internet. Experiment with the different styles and formats until you find one that you're most comfortable with.

EXAMPLES OF RÉSUMÉS/CVS

The following pages of CVs will be useful in helping you to write your own CV.

I have included my own one-page résumé, which I use to send to clients and editors, as an example of what can be squeezed into one page.

The other CVs are those of people who have been kind enough to offer them as examples. All have been disguised to 'protect' the individuals and companies concerned.

None of the examples is offered as a definitive example. All of them are unique to the people who wrote them. I hope that from each you will be able to take learning points to enable you to develop your own unique, personal and effective CV. Use the table below to help you. **Remember, it's YOUR CV, it's not a confessional! ... It's a marketing tool.**

Note: The CVs on the following pages have been printed on both sides of the page. Your CV should be single-sided to make it easier for employers to photocopy.

LEARNING POINTS FROM OTHER PEOPLE'S CVS

Things I like – to use in my own CV	Things I don't like – to avoid in my own CV

Malcolm Hornby
Résumé

Malcolm Hornby is Director of Delta Management, a consultancy which specialises in helping people to develop their teamwork, leadership and communication skills.

His previous experience includes:

Company Personnel Manager: Bristol-Myers Co. Ltd.

Managing the group's Personnel Department, providing a full personnel service to Bristol-Myers Pharmaceutical, Consumer and Clairol Companies on manufacturing, distribution and Head Office sites.

Company Training Manager: Bristol-Myers Co. Ltd.

Having company-wide responsibility for training and development at all levels.

Head of Sales Training: Eli Lilly & Co. Ltd.

Responsible for initial training and ongoing training of the sales force.

Other positions within Eli Lilly were:

Hospital Sales Manager – Managing a sales force selling pharmaceuticals to hospitals in the South of England.

Marketing Associate – responsible for market research and for developing sales and marketing plans.

Pharmaceutical Representative – selling pharmaceuticals to GPs, hospital doctors and pharmacists.

Previously Malcolm taught chemistry and biology in Liverpool and in Papua New Guinea with Voluntary Service Overseas.

He is tutor with the Open University's Business School, teaching Human Resource Strategies to MBA students, has published numerous articles on communication skills* and is the author of *3 easy steps to the job you want*.

Malcolm is a Fellow of the Chartered Institute of Personnel and Development and a Member of the Institute of Management.

Contact Delta Management: Tel +44 (0)1526 834666
www.DeltaMan.co.uk

* Published in: *The Institute of Training and Development Journal, Graduate Careers, Mind Your Own Business, Practice Management, The Journal of The Institute of Management Specialists, Managing Schools Today.*

STEVEN JOHNSON
22 Coventry Road, Egbaston
Birmingham B66 77BM
HOME TEL: (0303) 30303
E-mail Steven@Johnson.oc.ku

Highly motivated, energetic 44-year-old Senior Manager having successfully achieved objectives through developing people. A natural leader with strong interpersonal and communication skills who thrives on being involved in leading teams in an environment of creativity and constant challenge. Responsible for results of a keenly focused team in terms of Sales, Quality and Profitability. Displays initiative and a positive outlook to all challenges, ideas generator, decisive and highly adaptable to change. Extensive experience and knowledge of both general and sales management with an in-depth understanding of the people business.

ACHIEVEMENTS

Developed teams of managers monitoring both personal performance and that of the sales units, ensuring objectives achieved together with quality and service standards being maintained.

Created a competitive team spirit whereby individual and collective performance was recognised. Provided league tables, instigated competitions, produced interesting and varied communication formats.

Energised team, created environment ensuring national Sales Campaigns were tackled enthusiastically with success being achieved and measured in improving performance position.

Appointed and managed new Direct Sales Force including sales meetings, one-to-one coaching and field visits. Developed and nurtured relationships with sales units to achieve common business objectives, resulting in business levels being increased by 140% over a 6-month period.

Produced quarterly/annual business plans to ensure focus and direction to achieving business and quality objectives.

Instigated and developed a programme and systems for achieving Total Quality Management resulting in customer service complaints being reduced by 28% in 3 months.

Responsible for staff recruitment at junior management level. Disciplinary matters and general personnel responsibilities including managing staff budgets.

STEVEN JOHNSON ctd

Responsible for quarterly/annual appraisal process whereby individuals recognise critical success factors which are incorporated within a personal Development Plan.

Involved with the training of staff both within units and at Area Training Centre. Follow-up process adopted to ensure training benefits maximised.

Took part in strategic projects from inception to final presentation enabling project management skills to be developed to the full.

Conducted regular meetings and one-to-one discussions using consultative planning approach agreeing action points to ensure progress.

CAREER PROGRESSION   1975–present   Stable Building Society

2000 – present	Area Sales Manager Responsible for 16 Managers, 135 staff. Report to the Area Sales Director.	Midlands
1999 – 2000	Regional Sales Manager Responsible for 8 Managers, 4 Direct Sales.	East Midlands
1998 – 1999	Regional Manager	Coventry
1997 – 1998	Assistant Regional Manager	Coventry
1996 – 1997	Branch Manager	Harrogate
1989 – 1996	Branch Manager	Crewe
1983 – 1989	Branch Manager	Maidenhead
1975 – 1983	Junior Management/Senior Clerical	Various locations

PERSONAL DEVELOPMENT
March 1989   Sundridge Park Management Centre
November 1989   Peters Management Consultants (Sales Training)
December 1987   Ashridge Management College
                 Extensive Internal Training covering a wide range of topics.

ADDITIONAL INFORMATION
Married – 1 child (19)
Fellow Chartered Building Society Institute
School Governor/Chairman of Charitable Trust
Past member of Round Table, holding a number of offices including Chairman
Computer literate: all Microsoft Office Software packages

INTERESTS
Gardening, golf, badminton, stamp collecting, trying to keep fit.

PETER RADLETT
14 GREENVIEW
CENTRAL MILTON KEYNES
MK98 89MK
TEL: (987) 676767
E-mail: Peter@Radlett.oc.ku

CAREER PROFILE
Experienced and versatile manager with strong leadership skills. Knowledge
of high technology applied to a variety of product-based organisations.
Commercially aware. Adept at introducing change either in the
organisation or by the introduction of capital investment, and who
recognises that high productivity is only achieved through a
knowledgeable and motivated team.

ACHIEVEMENTS
* Implemented a £4 million investment programme on a greenfield site
  through the installation and commissioning of 4 discreet product lines
* Implemented capital investment programme to reduce reliance on
  external suppliers of key components
* Introduced the concept of Operator Process Control by use of a series of
  training modules
* Recruited, trained and motivated the production team to develop and
  grow the business
* Implemented new production planning routines to reduce generation of
  works documentation from 10 days to 4 days
* Reduced inventory holding on major product lines from 15 weeks to 5 weeks
* Developed, through training, line management supervision
* Reduced losses by improved monitoring and feedback to suppliers

CAREER HISTORY
2000 – Present   OPMKS Ltd, Milton Keynes – Manufacturing Manager,
                   responsible to Operations Director, for all aspects of
                   manufacture for photographic enlargers in a vertically
                   integrated organisation.

PETER RADLETT ctd

1999 – 2000	TISSUE Group, Hemel Hempstead – Production Manager, responsible to Operations Director, for all aspects of manufacture for Tissue Culture Products.
1997 – 1999	VENTILATORS Ltd, High Wycombe – Production Manager, responsible to Manufacturing Director, for line production, line planning and stock control.
1992 – 1997	HYDRAULIC MOTORS Ltd, High Wycombe – Manufacturing Manager, responsible to General Manager, for Purchasing, Production Planning, Stock Control, Production Engineering, Machining Assembly and Despatch.

EDUCATION AND QUALIFICATIONS

1980 – 1982	Hemel Hempstead Polytechnic – HND in Mechanical Engineering
1994	High Wycombe College of Further Education – Certificate in Computing Studies
1995	High Wycombe College of Further Education – Member, Institute of Industrial Managers (IIM)

MANAGEMENT TRAINING

1993	Guardian Business School – Accountancy for non-Financial Managers
1999–2000	Paradigm Shifters – Leadership and Decision-making Skills

INTERESTS
Squash, home improvements, computing, walking and classic cars.

ROBERT GREEN
IVYBRIDGE HOUSE
MANCHESTER ROAD
STALYBRIDGE
M99 99M
TEL: (669) 99991

****
An experienced Manager with Design, Technical and Sales skills. Has designed
numerous products including Bedroom/Kitchen ranges and Occasional furniture.
Prepared Technical Details of products including packaging. Handled numerous
Sales enquiries/contracts, liaising with clients at all levels. Assembled and fitted
products including Bedroom and Kitchen ranges.
****

ACHIEVEMENTS

*   Designed many successful products for mail order and high street clients
     including a new bedroom range by Bedroom Sellers and Housefitters.
*   Handled door contracts with national companies from enquiries through to
     production.
*   Designed and erected exhibition stands both in the UK and abroad.

EXPERIENCE

Bedrooms Ltd   1999 – Present
Manchester   Development Manager
Responsible for design and development of all the company's new products from
conception through to production. This involved accurate preparation of
production drawings using Autocad, material and fittings specifications, packing
design and instruction leaflets. On the sales side I handled all the company's
incoming door and component enquiries, liaising closely with customers on
technical matters. I had a staff of 5 and was responsible for CNC Programming
and the Development Workshop.

Components Ltd   1983 – 1999
Lancashire   Development Manager
Commenced my career as Design Draughtsperson working my way to
Development Manager on leaving. I was responsible for all aspects of design and
development work including aesthetic, economic and production considerations.
Was required to draw up and meet planning timetables; producing sketches and
cost for short-listed designs. Was involved with presentation and selling of

ROBERT GREEN ctd

product, pricing and quotations. I produced detailed customer assembly leaflets and was responsible for a busy development workshop.

Shell Oil Refinery	1980 – 1983
Cheshire	Process Operator

Responsible for efficient running of petrol refinery plant.
I gained experience in several different aspects of a Council department, including printing, preparation of art work, and furniture where I planned kitchen layouts for Domestic Science rooms in schools and colleges.

Bolton Borough Council	1975 – 1980
Bolton	Clerk/Draughtsman

I gained experience in several different aspects of a Council department, including printing, preparation of artwork, and furniture design. I planned kitchen layouts for Home Economics rooms in schools and colleges

EDUCATION AND TRAINING

Bolton Technical High School
GCE 'O' levels in English Language, Mathematics and Technical Drawing.

Manchester College of Furniture
Trained for Design and Construction of Furniture.

FIRA
Various day courses and seminars

College of Further Education
Bolton
City & Guilds in Computer Aided Draughting and Design using Autocad.

HOBBIES AND PASTIMES

I am a married man with two children. My interests include most sports but particularly fishing. I do a lot of walking, living close to moorland. I maintain and improve our house and do most of my own car maintenance.

CATHERINE SCARLET

14 Severn View

Bristol

BS99 9AA

Tel: 1234 56789 (home), 1234 98765 (office)

E-mail: Catherine@Scarlet.oc.ku

Finance Director with general management, company development and acquisition experience combined with practical operating skills in the Investment Banking, Broking, Chemical Processing and Retail Distribution industries. Special abilities include:

* Managing change; turning round underperforming activities.
* Forming, managing and motivating teams; developing individuals.
* Developing profitable relationships, negotiating business deals.
* Analysing, evaluating and managing company acquisitions.

CAREER LOTSACASH   INVESTMENT BANK GROUP

Operations Director, Capital Markets & Treasury, 1997 – present

Responsible for efficient operation of Capital Markets/Treasury financial control, settlements and computer operations. 100 staff, budget £10m.

* I was head-hunted to turn round ineffective accounting, computer and treasury control system.
* Re-built teams, improved staff quality and training, reduced staff and overtime without disruption, significantly improved management information and operating efficiency.
* Investigated and negotiated joint-venture arrangements in Europe.

BROKING INTERNATIONAL PLC, 1988 – 1997

Commercial Director, 1996 – 1997

Responsible for the London-based broking businesses. T/O £75m, profit £9m, 500 staff.

* Conducted start-up of German bond-broking business.

CATHERINE SCARLET ctd

Financial Director, Management and Securities Division, 1991 – 1996
Responsible for advising the Board on worldwide financial and related
management matters. T/O £113m, profit £22m. 90 staff.
*   Close involvement with acquisitions in UK, USA, Germany,
    Luxembourg, Hong Kong, Singapore and Australia and with subsequent
    business development.
Group Financial Controller, 1988 – 1991
*   Improved full range of management systems and controls in media
    advertising and broking activities.
    Contributions in the job led to promotion to Financial Director.

STACKEM HIGH STORES

Internal consultant, Retail Stores Division, 1987 – 1988
*   Investigated, recommended and implemented the integration of 2 stores
    groups.

SPRINGY SOFAS LTD

Managing Director, 1986
*   Planned and brought new factory to full production of moulded
    urethane components.
*   Developed market strategy and customer base of Group. T/O £3m,
    profit £160k.

QUALIFICATIONS

BA Accountancy and Law 2/1, University of Bristol 1978
CA gained with Price Waterhouse, 1981

PERSONAL

Age 46 years. Married, 2 children. Health excellent. Interests – family, antiques,
aerobics, Greek Mythology (launched and maintain special interest, internet
community website: www.GreekGeeks.co.uk)

JANET WAITE
58 Desmond Road
London
NW19 9DE
Tel: (020) 055 5656

PROFILE

An effective personnel generalist with skills in team-building and gaining commitment from Senior Management through persuasion.

Enjoys deadlines and performs well under pressure. Gives whole-hearted commitment to a task and displays a high degree of tenacity and resilience when facing difficult situations.

Outside of the work environment enjoys being stretched and, for example, has, in the last few years, taken up skiing, windsurfing and paragliding.

CAREER

VERY WEALTHY BANKS (INVESTMENTS) PLC   1986 – Present
(Based in the City with 2,500 employees in a highly IT-oriented environment).

PERSONNEL MANAGER   2000 – Present
SETTLEMENT SERVICES DIVISION
A strongly generalist role, responsible for the provision of an effective professional service to c900 staff. Managing a team of 6 personnel staff. My achievements in this role have been:
*   Following significant cutbacks, selected to contribute to re-structuring.
*   Charged with the task of detailed project planning and execution for the transfer of personnel activities back to line managers.

PERSONNEL MANAGER   1998 – 2000
INFORMATION TECHNOLOGY
Managing a team of 5 staff (including 3 professional personnel officers) covering strongly Systems Development oriented client areas, c550 staff. My achievements in this position were:
*   Worked with the senior management team to revise job roles and restructure a) the Systems Development and Support department resulting in the reduction of 30 staff and b) the Management Services department resulting in the reduction of 50 jobs.
*   Established a new personnel team of 5 from scratch; recruited, analysed training needs and coached for their improved job performance through regular meetings and improved communications. Heightened team contribution and helped them to develop in their own roles.
*   Implemented psychometric testing to determine analytical skills and assessment centre techniques to clarify project management potential, ensuring the cost effective application of training programmes.
*   Successfully implemented the appraisal policy within client area, running courses and successfully working to overcome management resistance to objective setting.

PRINCIPAL PERSONNEL OFFICER   1997 – 1998
BUSINESS DEVELOPMENT DEPARTMENT
In a predominantly Sales and Marketing environment managed 3 staff, in a generalist role serving staff in the South East, UK Regional Offices and New York, but also with emphasis on recruitment and remuneration.

JANET WAITE ctd

* Gained acceptance to the establishment of career paths for Business Development department staff involving progress through Customer Support, UK Sales, International Sales and the New York office.
* Creative and analytical approach to Recruitment into a number of key roles, according to a specification which required a unique combination of Financial Services, Computer Industry and Sales/Marketing expertise.

SENIOR PERSONNEL OFFICER   1996 – 1997
A generalist role, covering the Systems Development and Sales and Marketing department. Particularly involving recruitment and development (Graduate and YTS); and experience in HAY-based job evaluation. Achievements in this position were:
* Sold new salary review concepts to line managers and worked with them in resolving the remuneration level problems which were leading to high turnover of specialist staff.
* Initiated an in-house recruitment event to appeal to computer scientists, gained the commitment of the senior management to participate in the event and achieved recruitment targets.

BIG BOAT BUILDERS, RESEARCH & DEVELOPMENT   1994 – 1996
(Research, development and production of electronic equipment, 2,500 staff)

SENIOR PERSONNEL OFFICER – RECRUITMENT
Responsible for the recruitment of professional, technical, manual, clerical and secretarial staff. Involved in the recruitment of graduates and professional engineers. Achievements in the position were:
* Became the driving force behind the use of Psychometric Testing for the recruitment of specialist, high value staff. By means of presentations to Senior Management gained acceptance for this approach.
* Ran a series of 'walk-in interviews' to attract scarce technical skills and validated its cost effectiveness.

CAR PARTS LTD   1990-1994
(Manufacture and distribution of automotive parts, approx. 2,500 staff)
Successive appointments in this heavily unionised environment – Graduate JANET WAITE Ctd

Trainee, Salaries & Records Administrator, Personnel Officer, Systems Co-ordinator, Recruitment & Salaries Adviser.

ELECTRONIC SWITCHING LTD   1988 – 1989
Import/Export Sales Co-ordinator.

EDUCATION & TRAINING
Member of The Chartered Institute of Personnel & Development (1997)
BSc Combined Hons Degree in Science (Zoology/Geography)
Psychometric Testing
Registered user of ASE-NFER Nelson (all instruments), Kostic PAPI (Perception & Preference Inventory), Saville & Holdsworth (OPQ and Aptitude Tests)

PERSONAL
AGE: 36. Single. Interests include: Windsurfing, skiing, hill walking, watching motor racing, keep Siamese cats and enjoy theatre.

ACTIVITY (23)

Application forms

⟹ The mode in which the inevitable comes to pass is
through effort.   Oliver Wendell Holmes

What an imposition; you spend all that time writing your CV, spot an ad in the newspaper for a job that sounds perfect and you ring to ask for details. They send you an information pack and an application form. Why should you now waste time completing an application form?

It would be much easier to fill in your name and address at the top of the application form and write, 'please see attached CV' – you might get away with it, you probably won't!

Organisations use application forms for two main reasons:

1   To collect 'standard information' on all candidates, so that the person doing the initial screening can easily compare candidates against each other and the job.

2   So that candidates are 'forced' to provide important information, e.g. a CV may simply show 'full driving licence'. The response to a question on an application form, 'Give details of any driving licence endorsements', may reveal '9 penalty points; 3 x speeding'.

Looked at from one viewpoint, an application form is a chore; from a positive viewpoint, it is your perfectly targeted CV!

COMPLETING APPLICATION FORMS

- Read the form before writing anything.

- Take a photocopy of the blank form to use for drafting your answers.

- Complete the form as requested. Black ink and block capitals doesn't mean blue ink, no matter how dark, and hieroglyphics!

- If you need to expand any of the sections onto extra pages, write your name and job applied for at the top of each page.

- Match your application to the job: review the job advertisement and any information you have received on the job and match your application to the job.

- Answer all the questions.

- Explain any gaps in your career.

- Maximise the 'Other information' opportunity by making a positive 'you' statement – see Activity 31 'Selection interviews – Tell me about yourself' (page 188).

- Use feature and benefit statements to relate your past experience to the skills and qualities they are looking for – see Activity 24 'Selling myself'.

- Don't include any negatives about yourself – this is not the place to be self-effacing.

- Telephone referees before putting them on the application. First, as a courtesy, but second, to help them to help you by bringing out your best points when they give a reference. You want them to emphasise particularly those of your skills which are most relevant to the job.

- Proofread, proofread, proofread – and get someone else to do it.

- Photocopy the completed form – so that you know what you've said when you are invited for interview and to add to your brag box!

- Use first-class postage, or if the organisation is local, make an opportunity to 'be in the area' and deliver it by hand (in the same clothes that you would wear for an interview). You never know, you may even get a chance to meet the recruiter, or at least his or her secretary – an opportunity to make a positive impression, distinguish yourself from the competition and increase the memorability of your application!

ON-LINE APPLICATIONS

(See also Activity 29 'E-Jobsearching'.)

Take your time and be as thorough as you would if you were writing by hand.

Print off the questions and compose your replies to their questions in your word processor.

Read the advertisement and try to second-guess any special requirements or words that they'll be looking for. There's a good chance that your application will be scanned by special software, programmed to look for keywords and rejected if they aren't there.

When you're completely satisfied that you have got it right, and checked your spellings for the last time, go back on-line and copy and paste your text into their application form.

Final check and 'submit application'. You'll probably get an 'almost instant' E-mail acknowledgement. Don't get too excited. The software's programmed to do that as well. Good luck!

ACTIVITY (24)

Selling myself

➡ What we hope ever to do with ease, we must learn first to do with diligence.   Samuel Johnson

When you're actively job hunting you are constantly selling yourself whether by letter, telephone or in an interview.

Contrary to what you might think 'selling' isn't only about charm, a smile and a pleasant personality; these are part of it, but the selling process goes far beyond.

Most experts would agree that the basic core of any selling process involves the following:

Beforehand:

Objective setting   Identifying what you hope to get out of the contact.

During:

Presenting opening   Getting quickly to the point so that the other
benefits   person can see what's in it for them.

Probing for needs   Using 'How, Why, What, When, Where, and Who'
                            questions to help you understand requirements.

Presenting benefits   Helping the other person to see the relevance of what you
                            have to offer.

Overcoming objections   Outweighing any reservations they might have with the
                            benefits you can offer.

Closing   Ending the contact with an agreement of a positive
                            outcome.

PRESENTING BENEFITS

The process of presenting benefits is one which many people find difficult, so let's have a look at what's involved.

Features ➞ Advantages ➞ Benefits

People buy products or services not for what they are, but for what they can do for them. In the same way, companies recruit employees not for who or what they are, but for what they bring to the company and what they can do for the company.

WHAT'S THE BENEFIT OF BENEFITS?

I bought a mower with a 42" cutter deck, because it meant that I wouldn't have to waste too much time cutting the grass. BENEFIT – I can do other things that I enjoy doing!

I bought an answerphone with a remote interrogation facility, so that when I stay away from home, I can still keep in touch with my business contacts. BENEFIT – I keep in touch and don't miss out on business opportunities.

Benefit statements turn your gobbledygook into language which the other person can understand and is relevant to them.

By using benefit statements you will help the recruiter to understand any technical jargon you may be using and help them see the relevance of what you've done before the job you're being interviewed for.

Remember, in recruitment the recruiter is a 'customer' who is deciding whether to 'buy' your service for their company.

Feature	Advantage	Benefit
A description of product or service	Says what the feature does	Answers 'what's in it for me?'
A fact or characteristic	Says what the feature means	Answers what features and advantages will ultimately mean to user
A property or attribute of a product or service	Says what the feature will do	Gives the value of worth that the buyer will get from the product or service
'Because (of) ...'	'You can ...'	'Which means that ...'

The following exercises will help you to develop benefit statements for yourself.

Identifying benefits for a product/service

Choose something that you have bought recently. Write down four features in the 'Feature' section below. Now turn each feature into advantages and benefits (one feature can often give rise to a large number of benefits).

FEATURE What it is	ADVANTAGE What it does	BENEFIT
1		
2		
3		
4		
Because (of) …	You can …	Which means that …

Identifying benefits for me

Identify four of your achievements that you are proud of and write them in the 'Feature' section. Convert your features to advantages and benefits for your target job.

FEATURE What have I done? What are my achievements?	ADVANTAGE What I will be able to do	BENEFIT What it means to you
Because (of) …	You/I can …	Which means that …

At the end of each statement ask yourself, 'So what?' to challenge the relevance of what you say to the recruiter.

ACTIVITY (25)

Assertiveness and interpersonal skills

➡ Make the most of yourself, for that is all there is for you.   Ralph Waldo Emerson

Assertiveness skills are very important in many situations; by being assertive you are letting people know what you want, need or prefer in a way which is acceptable to both you and them. Put simply, assertiveness is about getting what you want without upsetting anyone!

In your jobsearch you'll need to be assertive if you're going to persuade people to give up time for networking interviews, send you company information or contact their contacts.

DIFFERENCES BETWEEN ACQUIESCENT, ASSERTIVE AND AGGRESSIVE BEHAVIOUR

Acquiescent	Assertive	Aggressive
You: hope that you will get what you want sit on your feelings rely on others to guess what you want	You: ask for what you want directly and openly ask for what you want appropriately have rights ask confidently and without undue anxiety	You: try to get what you want in any way that works often cause bad feelings in others threaten, cajole, manipulate, use sarcasm, conflict
You don't: ask for what you want express your feelings often get what you want upset people get noticed	You don't: violate other people's rights expect other people magically to know what you want freeze with anxiety	You don't: respect that other people have a right to get their needs met look for situations in which you both might be able to get what you want ('win-win situations')

Which column do you fit in for most of the time ... yes, I know everyone knows they should be in the centre column, but are you? If you aren't, set yourself three improvement goals to develop your assertiveness skills to help you to shift into the centre column.

Assertiveness goals

1 _____

2 _____

3 _____

Understanding and recognising assertiveness is a major step in helping you to develop your interpersonal and influencing skills.

There are two other important factors however:

1   How you prefer to behave with other people.

2   How the people you interact with like others to behave towards them.

For example, some people are the life and soul of the party, dress flamboyantly and speak in loud, fast voices; get two of them together and it's almost a competition to see who can burst the other's eardrums! Try approaching one of these people in a polite, mild-mannered and factual way and you're unlikely to make an impression.

Other people like to conduct business in a very formal way, they're abrupt and to the point and only interested in 'the bottom line'. Approach a meeting with these people with a barrage of questions about family, hobbies and what they did during the weekend, and you've probably burned up 80 per cent of the time they've allocated for the meeting!

SOCIAL STYLES

How can you ensure that you approach people in the correct way?

Knowing about 'social styles', developed by Merrill and Reid, is very useful. In the

Social Styles Model there are four basic 'styles' or preferred ways of interacting with others.

Merrill and Reid believe that a person's social style is a way of coping with others. People become most comfortable with that style, in themselves and others. Understanding your own style and those of others can help in making meetings more productive: the main objective of social styles is to help people to develop versatility in dealing with others.

A person's social style is measured in relation to three behavioural dimensions: assertiveness, responsiveness and versatility.

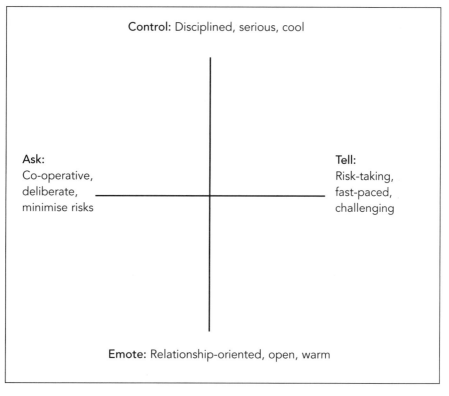

Control: Disciplined, serious, cool

Ask: Co-operative, deliberate, minimise risks

Tell: Risk-taking, fast-paced, challenging

Emote: Relationship-oriented, open, warm

Figure 2

The assertiveness scale

The assertive scale measures the degree to which a person is seen as attempting to influence the thoughts, decisions or actions of others, either directly by 'tell' behaviour or indirectly by questioning, 'ask' behaviour.

Tell behaviour: Risk-taking, fast-paced, challenging.

Ask behaviour: Co-operative, deliberate actions, minimising risks.

The responsiveness scale

The responsive scale measures the degree to which a person either openly expresses their feelings or controls their feelings. The ends of the scale are 'control' and 'emote'.

Control behaviour: Disciplined, serious, cool.

Emote behaviour: Relationship-oriented, open, warm.

The two scales combine to give a two-dimensional model of behaviour (Figure 2), which will help you to understand how you are perceived by others. The dimensions of behaviour will also help you to plan how you can deal more effectively with people of different social styles.

MY SOCIAL STYLE

To find out your own social style, tick the words below that give the best description of your behaviour. There are no right, wrong or 'best' answers:

A   Rexlaxed and warm   _____
     Opinions are important   _____
     Supportive   _____
     Flexible about time   _____
     Relationship orientated   _____
     Share feelings freely   _____
     Sensitive   _____
     Total ticks for A   _____

B Formal and proper _____

Facts are important _____

Controlling _____

Time disciplined _____

Task orientated _____

Keep feelings to yourself _____

Thinking orientated _____

Total ticks for B _____

Now subtract **A** from **B**, this may be a negative number e.g. if my **A** = 6 and **B** = 1 then my score is − 5. Plot your own score on the vertical (upright) arm of the social styles model.

X Avoid risk _____

Slow to make decsions _____

Passive _____

Easygoing _____

A good listener _____

Reserved _____

Keep opinions to yourself _____

Total ticks for X _____

Y Take risks _____

Swift decision _____

Direct _____

Impatient _____

Talkative _____

Outgoing _____

Express opinions readily _____

Total ticks for Y _____

Now subtract **X** from **Y**. Again, this may be a negative number e.g. if my **X** = 7 and **Y** = 3 then my score is − 4. Plot your score on the horizontal (flat) arm of the social styles model). (I'm actually a driver.)

Using my example with an **AB** score of − 5 and an **XY** score of − 4 my social style would be Amiable.

Now, join up two scores to identify your behaviour style.

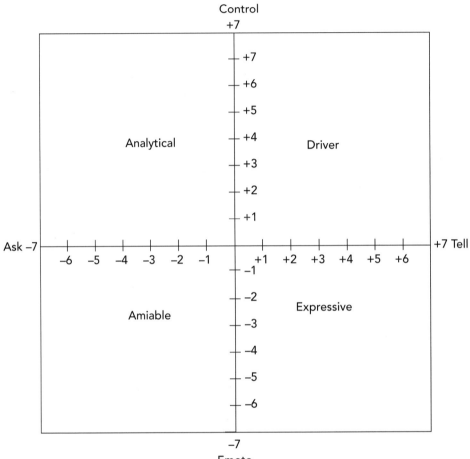

Figure 3 The social styles model

The social styles model is not about 'putting people into boxes', it is a way of plotting two dimensions of behaviour which then give us patterns to help our interpersonal skills.

By knowing about your own social style and recognising social styles in others you can improve the effectiveness of your meetings with others.

The table on page 157 summarises the characteristics of each of the social styles.

CHARACTERISTICS OF EACH SOCIAL STYLE

Analyticals	Drivers
• Concerned with being organised, having all the facts and being careful before taking action • Need is to be accurate and to be right • Precise, orderly and methodical, and conform to standard operating procedures, organisational rules, and historical ways of doing things • Have a slow reaction time and work more slowly and carefully than drivers • Perceived as serious, industrious, persistent, and exacting • Are task-oriented • Use facts and data • Tend to speak slowly • Lean back and use their hands infrequently • Do not make direct eye contact • Control their facial expressions • Others may see them as stuffy, indecisive, critical, picky and moralistic • Comfortable in positions in which they can check facts and figures and be sure they are right • Neat/well-organised offices • In times of stress, analyticals tend to avoid conflict	• Action and goal-oriented • Need to see results • Have a quick reaction time and are decisive, independent, disciplined, practical and efficient • Use facts and data • Speak and act quickly • Lean forward and point and make direct eye contact • Bodily posture is rigid • Controlled facial expressions • Do not want to waste time on personal talk or preliminaries and can be perceived by other styles as dominating or harsh and severe in pursuit of a goal • Comfortable in positions of power and control • Businesslike offices with certificates and commendations on the wall • In times of stress, drivers may become autocratic

Amiable	Expressives
• Need co-operation, personal security, and acceptance • Uncomfortable with and will avoid conflict • Value personal relationship, helping others, and being liked • Some amiables will sacrifice their own desires to win approval from others • Prefer to work with other people in a team effort, rather than individually • Have an unhurried reaction time and little concern with effecting change • Friendly, supportive, respectful, willing dependable and agreeable • Are people-oriented • Use opinions and stories rather than facts and data • Speak slowly and softly • Use more vocal inflection than drivers or analyticals • Lean back while talking and do not make direct eye contact • Have a casual posture and an animated expression • Perceived by other styles as comforting, unsure, pliable, dependent, and awkward • 'Homely' offices – family photographs, plants, etc • An amiable's reaction to stress is to comply with others.	• Enjoy involvement, excitement, and interpersonal action • Are sociable, stimulating, and enthusiastic and are good at involving and motivating others • Idea-oriented • Have little concern for routine and are future-oriented • Have a quick reaction time • Need to be accepted by others • Tend to be spontaneous, outgoing, energetic, and friendly • Focused on people rather than on tasks • Use opinions and stories rather than facts and data • Speak and act quickly; vary vocal inflection • Lean forward, point, and make direct eye contact • Use their hands when talking • Have a relaxed bodily posture and an animated expression. Their feelings often show in their faces • Perceived by others as excitable, impulsive, undisciplined, dramatic, manipulative, ambitious, overly reactive, and egotistical • Disorganised offices may have leisure equipment like golf clubs or tennis racquets • Under stressful conditions, expressives tend to resort to personal attack

VERSATILITY – MAKING SOCIAL STYLES WORK FOR YOU

First of all it is important to recognise that there is no best style. Merrill and Reid found that around 25 per cent of the adult population belonged to each social style. They also found people from each social style at all levels within organisations.

The third dimension and the key to using social styles is versatility. Statistically, around a quarter of the population have a similar social style to yours and so you will find that you are naturally comfortable with them.

Some people are naturally very versatile and are able to adapt easily to the needs of other people; others are less so. By developing your versatility skills, you will be able to relate effectively with a greater number of people.

The people whom you probably find it most difficult to relate to naturally are your 'diagonal opposites' on the matrix. Study the characteristics of your 'diagonally opposite' social style.

Make some notes in the box on p. 159 on how you can adapt your behaviour temporarily, i.e. improve your versatility next time you meet your 'diagonal opposite'. For example, analyticals may need to 'warm up' when dealing with expressives and be prepared to discuss business (network) over a pie and a pint or in the gym – just because the surroundings are informal doesn't make the information any less important. Expressives need to be specific in their contacts with analyticals; be precise about what you want and you'll find they have a wealth of knowledge, but give them time to gather it. Amiables need to get to the point quickly when dealing with drivers – all that chitchat about family and hobbies is lost on the driver. Similarly, the driver needs to slow things down when meeting an amiable in order to develop a trusting relationship.

Improving my versatility with my opposite social style:

1 _____

_____

_____

_____

2 _____

_____

_____

_____

3 _____

_____

_____

_____

THREE FINAL GOLDEN RULES

1   Person #1 is not person #2 – we are all different and individual.

2   Person #1 today is different from person #1 tomorrow – we all have our moods, both good and bad.

3   We can never know everything about a person or situation.

ACTIVITY 26

Active listening skills

➡ He who talks much cannot talk well.   Carlo Goldoni

Most of us are poor listeners … 'Sorry, did you say something …'? I said most of us are poor listeners!

We are so concerned with what we are going to ask or say, that we ignore or miss a lot of what the other person says.

Improving your active listening skills will help you to collect valuable information in your research interviews, when you're networking and when you are being interviewed for a job.

STAGES IN A NETWORKING INTERVIEW

1   Establish a relationship.

2   Encourage the other person to talk.

3   Reflect what the other person has said.

4   Summarise the key ideas you have got from the meeting.

5   Thank them for their time.

Look at the ten commandments of active listening on p. 161. How many 'sins' did you commit in your last networking interview?

THE TEN COMMANDMENTS OF ACTIVE LISTENING

1 JUDGEMENT EVALUATION – Thou shalt not judge or evaluate until thou has understood!

2 NON-CRITICAL INFERENCE – Thou shalt not infer thoughts, facts, or ideas in addition to those stated; avoid embellishment!

3 PLURAL INFERENCE – Thou shalt not attribute thine own thoughts and ideas to the speaker!

4 LACK OF ATTENTION – Thou shalt not permit thy thoughts to stray nor thy attention to wander!

5 ATTITUDE – Thou shalt not close thy mind to others!

6 WISHFUL HEARING – Thou shalt not permit thy heart to rule thy mind!

7 SEMANTICS – Thou shalt not interpret words and phrases except as they are interpreted by the speaker!

8 EXCESSIVE TALKING – Thou shalt not become infatuated with the sound of thine own voice!

9 LACK OF HUMILITY – Thou shalt not consider thyself too good to learn from any person!

10 FEAR – Thou shalt not fear improvement, correction or change!

IMPROVING YOUR ACTIVE LISTENING SKILLS

Non-verbal listening skills

You can communicate that you are actively listening by showing that you are paying full attention and not just waiting for your turn to speak, for example, by:

- looking at the person
- nodding your head
- facial expressions, e.g. raised eyebrows, a smile
- attentive body posture, e.g. sitting forward.

Verbal listening skills

There are a number of ways which will indicate clearly not only that you are listening but also interested in what the other person has to say:

- Rephrasing in your own words, e.g. 'So what you are saying is …'
- Summarising key points.
- Encouraging the other person to continue, e.g. 'That's interesting, tell me more.'
- Asking questions for further information or clarification, e.g:

> *Why do you say that?*
> *Why is that important to you?*
> *What do you mean by that?*
> *What does that mean to you?*
> *Would you explain that further?*
> *How does that relate to what you said before?*
> *Could you give me an example of that?*
> *Can you define or describe that?*

If you remember Rudyard Kipling's reply when he was asked how he came to develop such a wide knowledge, you won't go too far wrong. He said:

> *I keep six honest serving men*
> *(they taught me all I knew);*
> *Their names are **what** and **why** and **when!***
> *and **how** and **where** and **who.***

ATTITUDE

The chief requirement for active listening is to have 'room' for others; if we are preoccupied with our own thoughts, ideas and views, we are not mentally 'available' to listen effectively.

When listening, it is helpful really to try to understand the other person's view, without superimposing your own views or judgements prematurely – a major block to active listening.

Back to 'the ten commandments of active listening'!

ACTIVITY 27

First impressions that last

➡ There is new strength, repose of mind and inspiration in
fresh apparel.   Ella Wheeler Wilcox

When we communicate with people in a face-to-face setting we use two principal ways to transmit our message: words (content and voice tone) and body language.

Our 'word message' is made up from the words spoken and the way words are spoken.

The 'body language message' is the message we project through our gestures, actions and the way we dress.

Now, interviews are all about talking, usually one-to-one with another person, aren't they? You would be forgiven, then, for thinking that when you first meet someone you are going to capture their attention, provided that you have something interesting to talk about! It may surprise you to know that a number of studies have shown that the majority (around 80 per cent) of the messages we transmit to other people are through our body language.

We have spent a good deal of time throughout the rest of this book concentrating on what should be said in interviews. In this activity we will look at techniques you can use so that your body language projects the impression that you would want it to project.

STEREOTYPES

Whether you like it or not most people label others within the first few moments of meeting them. As much as 90 per cent of a person's impression of you is made in the first four minutes. Some of your initial impact comes from what you say but the majority of your impact comes from the way you behave and the way you dress – the other person stereotypes you.

To give you an example: in most western films what does the 'bad guy' look like? Moustache/unshaven, dark/black clothing and a black hat. He is easy to recognise – Lee Van Cleef hasn't played the part of a schoolteacher or parish priest, as far as I can remember, neither has Tommy Lee Jones!

In the classic Western, Butch Cassidy and the Sundance Kid confused our stereotyping by wearing camel-coloured clothes and being fresh-faced and clean-shaven (the slightly more villainous one wore a moustache). By breaking the stereotype, two outright criminals endeared themselves to millions of viewers.

Speak to most rational people and they will argue quite strongly that they 'always keep an open mind when they meet new people' and they are 'never quick to form an opinion'.

I understand the sentiment. In reality, I'm afraid it's not true.

Try this. Quickly imagine:

A secretary	now
A plumber	now
A school-meals assistant	now
A sales manager	now

What sexes were the people? What were they wearing?

Was the plumber wearing a dress or a skirt? Was the school-meals assistant wearing a suit, or was he wearing a blazer? Were you guilty of stereotyping?

You will stand a far better chance of getting the job you want if the image you project, through your body language, creates the right impact. In those vital first four minutes, you need to show that you fit into the stereotype.

I know that some people are very uncomfortable with what I have just said … 'What about freedom of choice' … 'No, I'm afraid what they see is what they get' … 'If they don't like me as I am then I'd rather go elsewhere.' If this is the way you feel then fine, I respect your opinions. What I will say, however, is that you may be shortening your options.

My target job

What is your stereotype of someone doing your target job? How do they behave? How are they dressed? What does their body language say? Make a few notes in the space below.

_____

_____

_____

POSITIVE IMPACT: BODY LANGUAGE

Dress yourself in a dark blue pinstriped suit, a white cotton shirt with double cuffs, a 'military' striped tie, black lace-up shoes and wear a plain-faced watch. (The woman's equivalent is the same with no tie, a white cotton blouse and black court shoes.) Your body language is about as persuasive and influential as your dress can let you be (No. 5 dress).

Studies carried out by IBM found that people dressed as I have just described were 40 per cent more believable than people who were 'less powerfully' dressed.

The less believable end of the scale is the camel-coloured suit, brown shoes and coloured shirt (No. 1 dress). While higher up come the light greys (No. 2 dress) with dark greys even higher (No. 3 dress). Watch the politicians and other public figures on television to see what effect the way they are dressed has on their 'believability quotient' with you.

It is impossible to generalise and give a definitive 'This is what you should wear for interviews', since all jobs have different requirements, but the following will be useful:

- Decide where on the 1–5 scale your dress should be appropriate to the job. Lovely as that new suit is (you know, the one you bought for your brother's wedding?), ask yourself if it is right for the job interview?

- Clean, well-pressed clothes in good repair – there aren't any buttons missing from the shirt/blouse you're planning to wear, are there?

- Wear some perfume or aftershave – but make sure it's not too overpowering. Be subtle.

- If you keep pets, brush your clothes thoroughly. Those cat hairs will start to look three feet long if you spot them on your clothes in the middle of an interview!

- Polish your shoes until you can see your face in them – not suede ones!

- If you're carrying a briefcase give it a polish.

- **For men:** earrings and white socks are a turn-off for most recruiters.

- **For women:** If you're wearing a new skirt, try the sit-down test when you buy it – is it too short? I once interviewed a young woman who sat through the whole interview with her top coat on her lap. She'd bought a new skirt for the interview and only realised how short it was when she sat down in it for the first time on the bus, on the way to the interview – too late!

- Beware of silk shirts and blouses – perspiration can really spoil their smart appearance.

- If you wear nail polish use 'neutral colours'.

- If you wear jewellery ask yourself if it is appropriate or too loud.

- Carry a spare pair of stockings/tights in your bag.

- Take only one bag with you into the interview. Fumbling between a handbag and a briefcase can make you look disorganised and reduces your confidence.

- *Colours:* A number of my friends have benefited from 'having their colours done', by taking advice on colours and tones to suit their skin and hair colour. The downside is that it's quite expensive – you may need to change your wardrobe! The positive side is that most of them feel it was beneficial. A cheaper alternative is a video, 'Discover Your Colours', details from our website www.TheJob-SearchersSuperstore.co.uk.

If you're leaving higher education, returning to work after a career break, switching career, such as leaving the armed forces or the police ... or making any career step that takes you into a new work culture, it really is worth giving careful thought to the image you want to project.

In addition to standing tall, smiling and being warm and friendly towards interviewers, the following will help you to send out positive messages.

- A handshake: rightly or wrongly, people read all kinds of interpretations into people's handshakes, from the limp lettuce, non-assertive, to the knuckle-crushing bully! A firm, but gently 'middle ground' handshake is usually appropriate to start and end interviews.

- Don't crowd the interviewer's personal space: In western society 4–6 feet is about as near as you should get to someone in an interview.

- Hold eye contact, but don't stare.

- Mirror the interviewer's body gestures: if the interviewer crosses their legs, do the same. If they raise their hand to their face, copy their gesture to produce a 'mirror image'. By this method you are telling the interviewer that you are in agreement with their ideas or attitudes. (Make sure that your mirroring is natural, otherwise mirroring will become mimicking!) If you want to observe mirroring, go along to your local pub or bar and watch people making each other feel relaxed by mirroring.

- Don't sit with your arms crossed: they form a physical block or barrier and send out an 'I don't believe you' message.

- Read the other person's body language:
  - Pulling or poking their ear – they've heard enough. Move on.
  - Hand clenching or clenching the chair arm – they're not impressed with your answer. Change the subject.
  - Readjusting their cuff/watch strap – they're bored. Move on.
  - Sitting back – they want to listen.
  - Leaning back with hands clasped behind the head – they want you to convince them.
  - Rubbing the chin suddenly – they're interested in what you're saying.
  - Index finger pointing up and resting on the cheek – they're evaluating what you're saying.
  - Leaning forward and rubbing hands together – they're very interested in what you're saying.

LAST IMPRESSIONS

A last impression from me!

Don't get so 'hung up' about gestures, actions and dress that you forget about the content of the interview! Watch people in real life or on television for examples of what I'm talking about.

When you attend an interview, a few well-chosen gestures and nicely matched attire will help you to create that perfect impression in the first four minutes.

ACTIVITY 28

The way in – finding vacant jobs

➡ The sleeping fox catches no poultry.   Benjamin Franklin

There are three kinds of job vacancies. Those which:

● already exist, someone has been promoted or left, etc.

● are about to exist, as a result of retirement or someone moving on or a company expansion

● are created, because your approach convinces the employer that there is a problem to be solved.

THERE ARE TWO WAYS OF JOBSEARCHING

Reactive: You read the vacancies sections in newspapers, journals and the vacancy boards of the job centre.

Estimates vary, but many believe that as few as 25 per cent of all job vacancies are ever advertised.

Proactive: You combine your Mulder and Scully investigative skills with your Anita Roddick/Richard Branson entrepreneurial skills to discover vacancies and market yourself so that you get the job.

Persistence and flexibility pay

When I was a 19-year-old student, I borrowed the airfare to the United States and enough money for me to exist on for 11 weeks from my parents. (Students do get long holidays don't they!) My travelling companion, Keith, and I arrived in Atlantic City, which is like Blackpool but around ten times bigger, in the middle of the holiday period. We had work permits and were sure that we'd be able to find jobs. We couldn't. American students start their summer holidays before the UK colleges. Every temporary job had gone. We spent three full days from 7.00 am until 10.00 pm calling at every hotel, restaurant, shop ... anywhere where we thought we could get work.

We took a bus to Philadelphia and spent another day doing the same thing there. But no luck.

We took a bus to Harrisburg. By mid-afternoon we had met a clerk at the employment offices who said there were no jobs in Harrisburg, but if we were interested in picking fruit he would take us that night to Gettysburg, where he knew there were jobs.

The next morning at 7.00 am we waited for the bus to arrive to take us to the fruit farm. It didn't arrive. It had been cancelled. No jobs.

The Gettysburg address I had was 3000 miles from home; we knew no one else and had just about enough money to survive for the rest of the trip! Back to knocking on doors. We also wrote a letter to the editor of the local newspaper saying how much we were enjoying our visit to the USA, but did anyone have any work?

In the meantime I managed to get a job – as a dishwasher at a Holiday Inn. Two days later our letter was published and a director of a shoe factory (who was English) rang to offer us jobs. Promotion! I resigned my job as a dishwasher and started at the shoe factory.

Two days after that, I received a call from a Howard Johnson Restaurant asking if I wanted a job as a cook. I explained that I had a daytime job, but was available during the evenings and at weekends. I started that evening.

I now had two jobs. A week later one of the other cooks resigned. I told the manager that Keith was available. He now had two jobs.

Persistence, flexibility, creativity and networking took the pair of us from being unemployed to giving us jobs that earned us enough money to repay our debts, finance our flights and an 11-week stay, which included a three-week, 11,000-mile tour of the USA!

Reading the appointments section in newspapers is an important part of jobsearching but there are many other ways.

PROACTIVE JOB SEARCHING

And there are two ways of proactive jobsearching!

Traditional techniques of proactive jobsearching

- Identify potential employers and write to a named person; not the personnel manager (unless you're looking for a personnel job), but the person running the department.

- To help in identifying potential employers take a trip to your local library and do some book research. There are literally dozens of directories. A quick phone call can re-confirm a name. When you know which geographical area, industry/public sector you are targeting, ask the librarian for advice on which directories will be most useful. The books will be in the reference section and some of the titles you will find useful will be:

The Personnel Manager's Year Book
Kompass Register of British Industry and Commerce
The Times 1000
Who Own Whom?
Stock Exchange Official Year Book
Directory of British Associations
Kelly's Manufacturers and Merchants Directories (regionalised)

And don't forget about the *Yellow Pages* and other local directories. And also the membership lists of professional bodies, e.g. the Institute of Chartered Accountants in England and Wales, the Law Society, the Institute of Taxation, etc.

There are also industry-specific directories, e.g. Pharmafile for healthcare industries. The list goes on and on – don't be put off. Ask for help and be prepared to do some digging!

- Write speculative letters to head-hunters and recruitment agencies. Build up your bank of names and addresses from friends and business contacts. Also, scan the newspapers and journals (current and previous editions) for people who work in your target area. An excellent source of names and addresses is the *CEPEC Recruitment Guide.*

- Contact the Branch Chairperson or Secretary of your professional organisation.

- Network: First of all, brainstorm the names of as many friends, acquaintances and business contacts as you can. Telephone them and get to the point quickly. Have three objectives:

  1   **To let them know that you're looking for work** – so that they can keep their eyes and ears open.

  2   **To ask them for the names of two of their contacts** whom you might approach.

  3   **To ask for their advice** about opportunities/recruitment consultants/ journals/ads they might have seen.

- Personal recommendation: if you have been made redundant, will your previous manager write to, or telephone, people in their network to ask if they will meet you? ... **Ask!**

GOYA techniques of proactive jobsearching

Get off Your A _ _ _!

- Be prepared to put in **a lot of effort**. Whatever effort you have planned to put into jobsearching, double it to a minimum of 20 hours per week and be prepared for a long journey. You need to put in some long hours. Be prepared to make dozens of phone calls and be prepared to write tens, or even hundreds, of letters of application.

- Target small companies. With a few exceptions, the big companies are contracting while **some** of the smaller ones are growing. Also, in a smaller company you're far more likely to get to see the decision-maker. Go there in person.

- Go to visit potential employers. Arrive in reception. Ask for the manager by name and be ready for a short interview; this is what salespeople call a speculative call – of course it doesn't work every time. But if you never do it, then it won't ever work. And you only need it to **really** work once, don't you! Be brave, try it!

- Aim to see ten employers each week, either through formal interviews or through speculative calls as described above.

- Visit your old school, college or university, nursing school, etc. People there may be aware of vacancies for people, with the skills or knowledge you have, or they may be able to give you names to add to your network.

- Have lots of 'irons in the fire'. Sometimes when people are jobsearching they 'fall in love' with one vacancy. As the interview process proceeds, they exclude any activity in looking for alternatives. It's almost as if there would be some kind of disloyalty to this potential job.

- Networking in person – wherever possible meet people face-to-face, rather than on the telephone: for a quick lunch, a meeting in the pub after work, or for a coffee. They'll give you ten times as much information in a one-to-one meeting as they will in a telephone call.

- If you've been shortlisted for a job and are attending a series of interviews put your heart and soul into it … but don't do it to the exclusion of all other activities. Keep jobsearching.

- Be creative, brainstorm! Try to think of novel and different techniques of finding out about new jobs. See if your friends can come up with different ways.

Can't be done – don't close your mind! Someone once found out my name and hand-delivered a nicely packaged box to the reception area of the company, where I worked as a personnel manager. The package was endorsed 'perishable – urgent'. It was delivered to me immediately, straight into my office (not buried in an in-tray) and placed on my desk. The contents: two packs of sandwiches from Marks & Spencer, a can of fresh orange juice, a cream cake and even a napkin. A letter in the box, from a young woman, explained that she realised I was a busy person; perhaps if she bought me lunch, the time I had saved could be spent giving her a short interview? When she telephoned me two days later, I spoke to her personally and met her a few days later. She had jumped in front of literally dozens of people. Regrettably, we didn't have any suitable vacancies. If we had, she would have been near the front of the queue … No, not because she bought lunch for me! But because she was prepared to try something different. It nearly worked. What she did get were some contact names of people in my network.

PS. I'm not suggesting that you now start to feed every potential recruiter! I am simply trying to demonstrate that there are merits in thinking creatively.

A friend of mine who is a partner in a law firm gave me this example.

'When recruiting for a solicitor we used a head-hunter, found an ideal candidate and he turned us down. Then I went to specialist agencies. Lots of CVs, interviews, etc. I turned down one person – not convinced she could develop the business enough. She wrote to me a couple of days later with her ideas for generating further business. I was impressed, had her back for a further interview and she got the job!'

If you have an interestng jobsearch method you have used, which has worked, write to me Malcolm@TheJobsearchersSuperstore.com or c/o Prentice Hall at the address on page ix so that we can share it with your fellow jobsearchers.

E-jobsearching: The internet has opened up so many opportunities. The whole of the next activity is dedicated to E-jobsearching.

You may be asking yourself, which jobsearching technique should I use?

My advice is: ALL OF THEM!

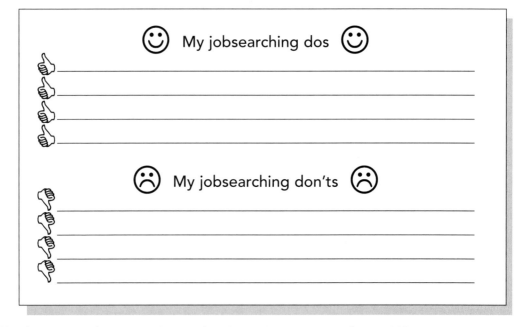

Use these notepads to summarise your learning points as you complete activities.

ACTIVITY 29

E-jobsearching

Finding a job using the internet

➤ The expectations of life depend on diligence; the carpenter that would perfect his work must first sharpen his tools.   Confucius

Since I wrote the first edition of this book the internet has seemingly permeated many aspects of most of our lives. It's a playground, a shopping mall, the best library in the world, and the quickest (and cheapest) way of obtaining and sending information that I know. E-commerce, the use of the internet in business, has well and truly come of age and it's still evolving. M-commerce combines the power of the internet with that of mobile communications and the latest development, P-commerce, adds on the ability of global positioning satellite (GPS) receivers to help you to locate wherever you are in the world. Very soon you will be able to drive to a new town and ask your on-board computer something like, who needs a personnel manager in this area? The three systems will combine to produce a list of local vacancies. Whether we need it or not it will soon be here. But for the moment, let's concentrate on the here and now and look at the internet.

It is not necessary to use the internet if you are looking for job. Not using it though says three things about you. The first is that you have not yet grasped the importance of the internet as a tool for accessing information. Second, you are restricting your career plans to people and places you are already familiar with. Third you are an ageing dinosaur crippled by technofear. (Tony Glover, writing in MicroScope, an IT journal)

Ouch! That hurts, but he's right. You CAN get a job without using the internet and many do, but using the Net in your jobsearch strategy you'll increase your chances of success. Some of the best sites have information exchange communities, careers advice and career-planning resources so that you can conduct your jobsearch all from one site.

As an experiment I have just used the *Times Educational Supplement* website to check for teaching jobs in Lincolnshire. Within less than 2 minutes I had an up-to-date list of vacancies! The power of the internet in your jobsearch gets even better!

Imagine being able to go to bed at night, and when you go back to your desk the next day your own private army of researchers have scoured trade publications, newspapers and journals. They have also phoned a few thousand recruitment agencies and employers, to find jobs that would be of interest to you. Sitting neatly on your desk is a small, but perfect pile of 'ideal job' vacancies! Well, your dreams have come true. Don't ask me how it works but the best sites have this facility.

When you register with them you can set up a process where their computer will automatically search their database each day to see if any new jobs match your criteria. You then receive an E-mail to notify you of the new job! To test the process I registered with www.Monster.co.uk and inputted my search criteria to my own jobsearch 'agent' two months ago. Since then, I have received notification of new jobs almost daily! What could be easier? There's no cost, so even if you're not actively looking for a job, you can sign up your 'search agents' and get E-mails, to keep your finger on the pulse of the job market.

But how do you go about using the internet in your jobsearch? A good starting point is www.TheJobSearchersSuperstore.com, the website of this book. You'll also find a directory of useful sites that I have checked in an appendix. But before you go on-line, read what the experts have to say.

I am extremely grateful to Simon Parker at Monster.co.uk and Andrew Banks and Geoff Morgan of TMP Worldwide for the following contributions. If you're new to the Net, their guidance should help you to understand just how important, and useful, effective use of the internet can be. (Monster is the leading internet website for jobsearchers. TMP Worldwide is a leading executive recruitment company with offices worldwide.) PS. Web, Net and internet all mean the same thing.

USING THE WEB TO SUCCEED IN YOUR JOBSEARCH

monster.co.uk

With thanks to Simon Parker, Marketing Director, Monster.co.uk.

Ideally, you want your jobsearch to take as little time and energy as possible, while producing optimum results. Sound impossible? It's not, especially if you use the Web to its best advantage.

THE IDEAL JOB SEARCH

The most successful jobsearch is a multi-faceted one. You want to achieve the right balance between research, preparation and action, while drawing from a mix of resources. Get it right and you'll expend less energy and vastly increase your chances of finding the right job that matches your needs and skills and allows you to grow professionally.

If you embark on a traditional job-hunt campaign, you may devote an excessive amount of time and effort that produces little reward. If your only jobsearching activity is checking the classified listings and sending out your CV to loads of organisations, you'll probably find yourself with a handful of interviews, at companies that may not be right for you, and have wasted a lot of time. By the same token you can greatly increase your chances by expanding your professional network, researching companies, and targeting organisations that are a good fit for your skills, interests and experience. Happily, in today's world, much of this work can be done on the Web.

What are the benefits of using the Web in career planning?

Recently, organisations and individuals have begun creating their own presence on the Net. This means there's a countless amount of information for you to access. At the same time, too many choices can be overwhelming.

CONVENIENCE, FLEXIBILITY AND COST EFFICIENCY

You can access the Web at any time of day or night. Having your own computer and internet access means you can also conduct a good deal of your jobsearch on your own time scale and in the comfort of your own home. Also, because Web resources are categorised and searchable by keywords, you can broaden or narrow your focus as you choose and access large amounts of information easily and efficiently. Links between and within sites enable you to pick and choose your direction, providing a non-linear approach to information-gathering. That means you can navigate multiple sources of information with ease and go directly to the source that most appeals to you. In addition, the Web provides a cost-effective means to access information from all over the world about job-related issues. It's relatively cheap (even free at many universities) to access the Web, and once you do, the information is free.

So what career resources are out there, and how can a job seeker effectively use the Web?

INFORMATION AND PREPARATION

Businesses, professional and industry associations, career-planning tools, career fairs, job listings – they're all on the Web, so it makes sense that you should be visiting them.

Many businesses have their own sites where you can find basic background information, an understanding of their role in their industry, a glimpse of the corporate culture, job opportunities, contact information and more. Some sites provide company data on a multitude of organisations; others provide detailed financial information through annual reports. You can look up industry information, trends and job prospects through government sites, professional associations and industry guides. There are a number of employment guides that provide employment statistics, useful articles and links to other job-related sites. The Web is full of directories of career and job fairs, electronic job listings and classifieds that you can search by location and keywords. Regional and relocation information can be found on-line through local, regional and national sites such as local councils, tourist information offices, government sites. On-line magazines also provide this information with searchable directories and reviews of various cities and countries.

COMMUNICATION AND GUIDANCE

Since the internet is a massive network, what better place to do your networking? After all, networking is the single most effective means of finding a job. Whether you want advice, to arrange networking and informational interview opportunities, or to respond to an ad or job posting, people around the world are available on-line through their sites and through E-mail, mailing lists, bulletin boards and Web conferencing. The Net's a friendly place. Because of its interactive nature, you can contact business people, non-profit people, career professionals and placement offices, professional associations and special interest groups, fellow students and job seekers, and even employment support groups.

UNIVERSITY AND COLLEGE SITES

Many university career offices and placement offices have their own sites on-line, and they are a great source of career-related information, particularly for students, recent graduates, new job-hunters, and even career changers. If you're a student you can access information from your own university's career centre, but feel free to visit other university sites as well. These sites generally contain a wealth of information ranging from self-assessment tools to CV and interview preparation tips to campus interview schedules to job listings. Most also offer descriptions of other worthy career-related sites and provide links to them.

SPECIAL INTEREST SITES

Professional associations and other specialised groups have valuable career-related information. These range from outreach groups, that help to employ a particular segment of society, such as women in business, to others that help people with disabilities. There are sites for racial and ethnic groups, for part-time workers, and many more. These sites can be excellent for information-gathering and networking.

Some self-assessment testing organisations offer their services on-line to help you evaluate your own skills, interests and values so that you can better focus your career goals.

ADVICE AND INSIDER INFORMATION

Professional associations and career specialists are on-line all over the world, providing information on employment and particular industries. Most information is already posted on-line, with other information on request. On-line career columns enable you to submit your questions and receive answers on-line and through E-mail. There are also mailing lists to which you can subscribe that enable you to communicate with a large number of people, all of whom are interested in the same subject as you and some of whom are experts in the field. You can subscribe to one or more of them to ask questions, increase your network, or even just to be a fly on the wall and observe what's going on in your field of interest.

You can also participate in Web conferences and post your requests, questions, concerns, CVs, job postings, and more on electronic bulletin boards, and people will respond, sometimes even directly to you.

TO GET THE BEST OUT OF THE NET

Know thyself: Do some self-exploration on the Web

Consult self-assessment resources, career and placement centres; read and conduct informational interviews; seek advice through professional associations, E-mail, bulletin boards and mailing lists. Many of these resources can also help you develop important career-planning and job-hunting skills such as writing CVs and cover letters, preparing for interviews, and learning appropriate business terminology and etiquette for different professions.

Know thy target: Gather company, industry and regional information

Discover viable occupations and industries that match your skills through government sites, industry sites and on-line career magazines that offer detailed descriptions of different professions through articles, statistics and searchable databases. Explore employment possibilities and quality-of-life information for a given city or country by searching government, travel and relocation-related sites. Research prospective target organisations by accessing company home pages and searching company databases.

Make contact

Locate career, business and industry professionals through their respective websites, E-mail, bulletin boards and mailing lists. You can learn more about their businesses and your options, increase your network and pursue job leads.

Go forth and conquer!

The final key to enhancing your jobsearch is striking the balance between being inquisitive and efficient in your research. One of the most rewarding aspects of using the Web is its exploration. Be systematic, and don't be daunted. Just remember that the information is out there waiting for you, and it's important to strike a balance between setting your agenda and sticking to it while still allowing yourself to take advantage of the unknown prize lurking behind Link Number Three. Good luck in your search!

tmp.worldwide | MAXIMISING YOUR USE OF THE NET IN YOUR JOBSEARCH

Andrew Banks and Geoff Morgan, TMP Worldwide – Executive Resourcing.

The on-line world is rapidly becoming the easiest way to search and apply for jobs 24 hours a day, seven days a week, without geographic or time barriers.

As the internet and on-line population is now greater than the population of many countries, employers and employees alike are flocking to on-line recruitment and networking.

BUILDING A CV

The reason recruiters and many employers want to receive your CV electronically is because they will store your details electronically in a candidate database. This allows them to search and match your skills against the positions they have vacant instantly.

There are a few basic rules to remember when building an electronic CV:

● Always create as plain text or ASCII, e.g. if the employer only has Word Version 3 and you create a Word Version 6 file, the employer will not be able to open the file.

- Do not underline headings.
- Do not use italics unnecessarily.
- Do not use tables unnecessarily.
- Always format in portrait style.
- Do not include graphics or photographs of yourself.

If all of the above appears too complicated there are some web sites that offer CV-building facilities. These services should always be free of charge. They are designed to assist you to build a professional on-line CV that is user friendly, highlights key words and is in a format that is accepted by almost all employers. The one exception to this rule is government organisations, where you are usually expected to fill out a standard government on-line application.

THE DON'TS OF ON-LINE JOBSEARCH

- Don't send a general CV without a cover letter stating where and when you are available for work and, most important, what type of job you are seeking.
- Don't send your CV on an E-mail to multiple organisations. Remember, the top of every E-mail you send will show whom else you have sent your details to. Mass E-mails do not create a good impression.
- Don't ask general questions like, 'How do I get a job?' or 'Do you have job vacancies?'. Be more specific and remember you may be one of thousands of E-mails that an organisation receives weekly. The more specific your question the more specific the answer.
- Don't E-mail your CV to a prospective employer or recruitment firm in the latest WP version. Often the most basic is best, for example, a basic text file (.txt) is likely to be accessible by all versions of computer users. While sending your CV in the latest version of Word may make you think you are technologically up-to-date, it will simply frustrate the potential employer if they are unable to access your document.

THE DOS OF ELECTRONIC APPLICATIONS

- Do use key words that show you match the position requirements.

- Do keep the CV short and sharp. Remember, it is an initial contact only.

- Do put your most important skills at the beginning of the CV.

- Do keep the format of the CV simple.

- Do use only plain fonts, no italics or underline and no borders.

- Do remember to provide your E-mail address and telephone number. The aim is to be contactable, so make sure your E-mail address is correct on your CV.

- Do always keep a hard copy of your CV close at hand for incoming enquiries.

REASONS TO USE THE INTERNET IN YOUR JOBSEARCH

- Free access to information and resources: With access costs to the internet becoming more and more competitive, more people are beginning to take advantage of the thousands of free resources and job listings, as well as CV writing tips, interview tips and other career guidance tools.

- Use key words to find jobs: Newspapers provide job listings; however, they can require extensive visual scanning. The internet, by way of contrast, allows you to search job databases using key words for fast, effective retrieval of jobs.

- Access to company vacancies: The majority of large companies now provide a set page on their website dedicated to vacancies within their organisation, or provide a direct link to their HR department. Many of these vacancies are company-wide and are not geographically restricted.

- Networking: The most important part of getting a job is making contacts and where best to do so than on the world's largest electronic network!

- Tomorrow's information today: While newspapers publish a job section on a weekly basis, and the information published is only valid as to the day of print, the internet provides you with daily updates of vacancies worldwide.

- No boundaries! The internet has no geographic or time barriers, and access is available 24 hours a day, 365 days a year.

- Leading-edge skills: Organisations, especially businesses, are rushing to get onto the internet. They see opportunities for advertising, possible commercial markets and a vast wealth of information that they can tap into. Using the internet in your jobsearch demonstrates to the employer your familiarity and skill with this new market area.

- Searching for jobs using global technology: There is more to searching for a job on the internet than giving it to a large on-line job bank/employment page. You need to have a plan of attack. There are some specific job-related web pages on the internet that you can use to source the job you are looking for. These are as follows:

  - Recruitment websites: A home page for a recruitment firm will display general or industry-specific jobs for you to view. A recruitment website of merit will provide you with the ability to apply for positions on-line.

  - Employment jobs bank: An employment jobs bank represents a site on the internet where both recruitment firms and employers can post job vacancies. A usual service provided by some jobs banks allows you to post your CV in a secure area, so only employers and recruitment firms of your choice can view your details.

  - On-line classified: An on-line classified website is what we refer to as a newspaper on-line. Many of the major newspapers now sport their own website displaying employment adverts that they have printed in the press. If you apply to a classified website your CV will normally be directed to the recruitment firm or employer who has placed that particular vacancy.

  - Company home pages.

  - Electronic journals: Electronic journals are industry-based publications normally managed by a society or organisation. These are usually free and provide industry-related articles and possible networking contacts together with job listings.

  - News groups: internet news groups are public bulletin boards where you are free to post requests for employment or vacancies. The jobs news groups have jobs, CVs, discussions on how to find a job, and general career information. Industry-specific news groups provide an excellent opportunity for networking. (For a comprehensive list of news groups go to http:\\www.listz.com.)

- Mailing lists: Similar to news groups, mailing lists cover a broad variety of topics and industries. Occasionally, job postings can be found. However, their main benefit is to establish networking contacts, keep abreast of industry trends and receive updates on who's who in a specific industry.

● Search engines: enter key words; use subject categories; assess recruitment sites through banner advertising.

SOME WORDS OF CAUTION

Now you have read the experts' advice, some words of caution. Let me ask. Would you stand naked in the centre of your local city, shouting to the world that you're looking for a new job and carrying a placard displaying your address, phone number, earnings, medical history, age and sex of your children … etc.? No, I didn't think you would! Watch out that you don't do the electronic equivalent on the Net. internet users reflect society and while most people are honest and decent, some are not. Beware of what you tell to whom. Once you have given out information, you can't get it back! Check out the credibility of internet recruiters and don't reveal personal details in chatrooms, communities and newsgroups.

TO END ON A POSITIVE NOTE

I believe that the internet is the most significant technological development of modern times. Seize its power, grab your mouse and come surfing!

Understanding selection criteria

➡ Nothing is really work unless you would rather be doing
something else.   James Matthew Barrie

Present yourself well in an interview and you're probably 95 per cent of the way to getting the job! So, how do you do it?

Good interviewers work to a plan, using questions to measure/assess you against their ideal profile. They set standards/requirements relating to a variety of factors and decide if these are essential or desirable. The chart on page 187 shows a typical 'Person profile form', used by many recruiters.

HOW THE SELECTION CRITERIA ARE USED

When planning a recruitment project a recruiter will use the 'person profile' like a shopping list to try to help them to identify what the IDEAL candidate should be like.

For example, someone selecting a marketing executive might decide that it is essential that the person should be of graduate level and desirable that they should have an upper second class honours degree. They may decide that it is essential that the person has very good interpersonal skills since they will be working with a variety of people, etc.

Some information is easy to establish such as exam grades, while other information, such as interpersonal skills, involves judgement and evaluation of your answers to questions.

Like many other decisions in life, recruitment decisions are often a compromise. The person profile is the recruiter's shopping list to help them to identify the ideal candidate. When you are applying for jobs, work out 'what would be your ideal candidate for the job' if you were recruiting. What would you be looking for? Use the 'person profile' as a checklist.

Person profile	Essential	Desirable
Physical make-up: height/build, appearance, health, speech, etc.		
Attainments: education, qualifications, training, work achievements		
General intelligence: ability to sustain a logical argument, common sense, creativity		
Special aptitudes: numeracy, literacy, creativity, mechanical aptitude, dexterity, etc.		
Interests: political, social, active outdoor, practical, intellectual, etc.		
Disposition: interpersonal relationships, influence over others, industry, self-control, self-reliance, dependability, etc.		
Circumstances: family and domestic, willingness to relocate, willingness to travel, etc.		
Motivation: why this job – has the person got the 'can do' and 'will do'?		

ACTIVITY 31

Selection interviews

> When you have spoken the word, it reigns over you. When it is unspoken, you reign over it.   Arabian proverb

HOW YOU CAN PREPARE

The FBI say 'proper preparation and practice prevent a poor performance'. Prepare carefully and practise thoroughly for your interview. You will increase your confidence and your chances. Don't rely on charm and wit, there's too much at stake. Interviewers like well-prepared candidates, who show a genuine interest.

Find out what you can about the job, the organisation, its products or services. Visit the website. Get a copy of the annual report (if it's a PLC they have to provide an annual report when requested) and product literature – getting a youngster to telephone the public relations department for a 'school project' is a good technique if you feel uncomfortable asking (although most people will view it positively if you request additional information). Research into the type of company; public, private, family owned, etc. – its performance compared with competitors, etc.

If you can, talk to people who use the company's products; a friend of mine who applied for a job selling surgical devices spent a day in an operating theatre seeing the products in use. All he did was to ask the surgeon whether he could – yes, he got the job! Now he's their Managing Director in Australia!

Get a copy of the job description if you can. If you can't, ask yourself why not? There may be a perfectly good reason or it may be that they haven't yet decided what your duties will be – a potential source of discontent for the future!

Re-read the advertisement, your application (you did remember to photocopy it before you posted it?) and your CV. Highlight what you can offer to match their requirements. Bear in mind that when companies recruit they rarely get a 'hand in glove' fit with a candidate who matches their requirements exactly. Your aim is to convince them that you are the best match.

Now is the time to cast modesty aside. It is almost certain that you will be asked something like, 'Tell me about yourself' or 'What can you offer to our organisation?'.

'Tell me about yourself'

Before the interview, write a short 'You' statement (below) which answers these questions, making five or six positive statements (remember to include benefits) about yourself. Focus especially on your work skills. If you have completed the earlier activities this step should be straightforward.

Positive statement

1 |_____

2 |_____

3 |_____

4 |_____

5 |_____

6 |_____

Now practise saying it – yes, I know it feels uncomfortable but it is worth it, because it does work.

Practise the interview with a friend who is prepared to give you some feedback. Use a tape recorder or video camera (available on hire from many electrical stores and often cheap to rent midweek) to hear/see yourself as others do. Don't be despondent; we are all our own greatest critics and your accent isn't really that noticeable!

Are you up-to-date with developments in your field – scan the trade journals and the Net. You don't have to be a guru to be informed.

If you can, find out who will be interviewing you – think about what they might be looking for. This is particularly important if you are applying for a promotion or you already know the organisation well.

Decide an acceptable financial package – but let the interviewer raise it.

Plan your journey. There is virtually no excuse for being late for an interview. Allow extra time for rush-hour traffic, road works, and finding a parking space.

INTERVIEW DAY

Dress smartly in well-pressed, comfortable clothes appropriate to the job/organisation. Get your hair trimmed. Do what you can to make yourself feel good – if you feel good inside, you'll present yourself well on the outside.

Arrive early so that you can prepare yourself. Admiral Horatio Nelson is reputed to have said, 'I owe my success in life to always being 15 minutes before my time.' I can't vouch for the accuracy of the statement, but the principle is sound! Don't arrive more than 15 minutes before the interview, however – wait outside. Some people see arriving much too early as poor time-management. They may be embarrassed to keep you waiting for a long time.

When you speak with receptionists and secretaries, remember they may be asked for their comments, as may the person who gave you an 'informal' tour of the site or offices before the interview.

Look around: could you work in these conditions, do people seem comfortable talking to each other, what is your impression of the culture? If you prefer a formal working environment where everyone is Mr or Ms etc., and you hear first names being used, the culture may not be right for you, and vice versa.

Leave the raincoat and umbrella in reception, so that you'll arrive at the interview uncluttered.

THE INTERVIEW

Smile and shake hands firmly, if the interviewer offers their hand.

Wait to be invited to sit down. If the wait seems too long ask, 'Where would you like me to sit?'

If you're offered a drink, accept it. Even if you only take one or two sips, it will be very useful if your throat starts to dry up.

Remember, you are well on the way to a job offer. The interviewer hopes you're the right person!

Take a few deep breaths, relax and be natural. This is your opportunity to show the interviewer that you are the person they're looking for.

Sit well back into your chair, in an upright but comfortable position. If you use your hands when talking, be aware of it and don't overdo it. Make friendly eye contact with the person asking questions. Don't stare. If you feel uncomfortable holding eye contact with people, look at the point of their forehead just above the nose – it works, honestly. If there is more than one interviewer, make sure you also involve them by addressing the next part of your answer to them. For panel interviews address the main body of an answer to the questioner, but then hold eye contact with other panel members in order to involve them. Only use the interviewer's first name if they invite you to.

Brevity is the essence of good communication. Pause briefly for a second to think before you speak. Don't ramble, wasting valuable time. The interviewer is more interested in the quality of your answer than the quantity! Don't waste too much time either talking about your early career; your recent achievements are usually far more relevant.

Listen actively to what is being asked or said – if you need to get a better understanding repeat or rephrase their question.

Be prepared for questions the interviewer knows you'll find difficult to answer, such as ones about a controversial subject. These are asked to see how you respond under pressure. Don't blurt out the answer; a short pause shows thoughtfulness.

Stress what it is about your skills and achievements that makes you the person for the job.

Introduce those five or six key 'You' points using benefit statements (see also Activity 24 'Selling myself' on page 147). Help the interviewer to see how your skills and experience will benefit their organisation. It will be too late if you remember when you're half-way home!

If the interviewer is your potential manager ask yourself whether you will be able to work with him or her.

Have a notepad and pen handy in your bag, pocket or briefcase to take any notes and answers to your questions at the end. This shows you have thought about the job. Questions you might like to use are shown near the end of this section.

Thank the interviewer and ask about the next step. This confirms your interest in the job.

Avoid:

- Smoking, even if the interviewer is.

- Showing references, job descriptions or samples of your work unless asked.

- Criticising employers and long stories about why you left jobs, particularly if you have a grievance with a previous employer.

- Talking about personal and domestic matters, unless asked.

- Getting on your soap box. What you do in your own time is of little concern to most employers, but few like activists or shop-floor politicians at work. Practise courteous answers to any likely questions.

- Raising salary/package. Let them know what you can do; this may well influence their view of what you are worth. Usually employers have a salary range in mind. If you ask about money too early they will give the lower figure. How many people do you know who have gone shopping to buy, say, a hi-fi system with a price in mind of £500–£650 only to find that they buy one for £725? The same happens in recruitment.

- Name-dropping. It can backfire!

- Interrupting the interviewer in your enthusiasm to make all your points.

- Pretending you've got a better offer elsewhere to try to push them into a decision. But do let them know if you're being interviewed by other people – it can sometimes focus their minds! They don't want to miss you and don't give away too much information.

PREPARING FOR THEIR QUESTIONS

You can't know what is going to be asked but you can improve your chances by practising some common questions – ideally with a friend.

Start off with 'Tell me about yourself'. (Initial nervousness may cause you to say too much – don't.)

If you're asked to talk about your career history and you've had a variety of jobs, don't dwell on your early career; the interview will have been scheduled for a set time and it is usually more important to talk about current/most recent responsibilities and achievements.

Now try answering some of the questions shown below. Paint the best image of yourself and show what you have to offer by talking about your skills and achievements.

Why did you leave …?

How are/were … as employers?

What makes a good employer?

What have you been doing since you left …?

What did you enjoy doing at …?

What are your greatest strengths (weaknesses) as an employee?

What have been your best achievements?

What are the qualities needed in a good (job title)?

What qualities do you look for when recruiting subordinates?

If we offer you a job, what can you bring to our organisation?

What area of work do you feel least confident about?

What do your colleagues/manager see as your greatest weaknesses?

How would you describe your career progress to date?

What have you learned in your time with …?

What do you see yourself doing in 5/10/15 years?

Why did you become a (job title)?

How do you take direction?

How do you spend your holidays?

Have you ever been dismissed (disciplined)? Tell me about it.

How is your health?

How many days sick leave have you taken in the last two years?

How do you relax?

What do you know about our company?

Why do you want this job?

Why should we offer you this job?

Are you being interviewed for any other jobs?

Which do you want?

Some interviewers ask hypothetical questions along the lines of, 'How do you think you would react in … situation?'. Here you find yourself 'second-guessing' them by saying how you would behave, in the way you think they want to hear! It can become quite an amusing game!

Other interviewers ask questions about what you have done in the past, since this is their best indicator of how you may perform in the future. They are looking for you to have handled situations in a positive way and for you to have learned from experience. Help them by:

- Describing the situation and what had to be done.

- Explaining what you did.

- Describing the outcome in positive terms.

Practise answering some of the questions below. They seem simple but are very searching!

Questions about your effort/initiative

Tell me about a project you initiated. What prompted you to begin it?

Give an example of when you did more than was required.

Given an example of when you worked the hardest and felt the greatest sense of achievement.

Planning and organising skills

What did you do to get ready for this interview?

How do you decide priorities in planning your time?

Give examples.

What are your objectives for this year? What are you doing to achieve them? How are you progressing?

Interpersonal skills

Describe a situation where you wished you'd acted differently with someone at work. What did you do? What happened?

Can you describe a situation where you found yourself dealing with someone whom you felt was over-sensitive. How did you handle it?

What unpopular decisions have you recently made? How did people respond? How did that make you feel?

Sales ability/persuasiveness

What are some of the best ideas you ever sold a superior/subordinate? What was your approach? Why did it succeed/fail?

Describe your most satisfying (disappointing) experience in attempting to gain support for an idea or proposal.

Decision-making

What are the most important decisions you have made in the last year? How did you make them? What alternatives did you consider?

Describe an occasion when you involved others in your decision-making. To what extent did you take notice of their input?

Leadership skills

What are some of the most difficult one-to-one meetings you have had with colleagues? Why were they difficult?

Have you been a member of a group where two of the members did not work well together? What did you do to get them to do so?

What do you do to set an example for others?

YOUR OWN QUESTIONS

Remember the recruitment interview is a two-way process. You may be making a choice about where you will spend the rest of your working life. Make the most of your opportunity to find out what you need to know and also to create a business-like impression. Start with questions which show an interest in the job, not what the company can do for you.

Make a note of what you want to ask beforehand and if you need to, take brief notes of the answers. Examples of information you might like to gather (but not all at once!) could be:

The job

What will be your daily responsibilities/duties?

What is the level of the job within the company's grading structure?

To whom does the job report?

Is there a job description/what are the main priorities?

Reporting – up/down/sideways – are there any dotted-line responsibilities?

What will be your budget availability?

What are relationships like with other departments?

What are the people like for whom you would be responsible? Are there any 'management' issues?

In what way is the company committed to your own training and development?

What are the opportunities for progress/career advancement?

What resources would you have available to help you achieve your goals?

The company

What is the UK/total turnover?

Is there a statement on company philosophy/mission statement?

What is the company's profitability compared with competitors/budget?

How big is the workforce/turnover (of staff)?

What is the range of UK services/products?

What is the company's E-commerce strategy?

What new products/services are under development?

What innovative ways are used to market their products/services?

Where will the company be in 5/10 years?

The practicalities (questions for when you are on the home straight!) (when considering their offer keep the total package in mind)

Medical – is it required?

Start date – how soon?

Pension – how is the scheme structured? Can you transfer in?

Salary review – based on what? How often? When will your first one be?

Car – allocation/running costs or charge?

Average salary increase last year/previous years (how is it reviewed)?

Holidays?

Private healthcare – is it available? How much does it cost? Are spouse/family covered?

Insurance – what is the company scheme?

Bonus scheme – what is the structure?

Share options – are they available?

Salary – where does the figure they have offered fit in on their salary scales?

AFTERWARDS

Relax and congratulate yourself on having been as well-prepared as you could be. Reflect on how it went and write down key points which could be important in a next interview.

You'll probably have to wait to hear their decision, but you can learn from the experience.

Were you happy with the way you handled yourself? Did you get across what you wanted to? Did you find out what you needed to know?

How many of 'you' points did you get across?

Was your behaviour positive, assertive, humble, tense, laid-back, talkative, controlled, etc.?

If you've been put forward by a recruitment agency, call them as soon as you can to let them know how you got on and to confirm your interest in the job. They will almost certainly feed this straight back to the interviewer and it will be viewed positively. Otherwise, leave the ball in the court of the interviewer.

Don't become too despondent if you don't hear for a while – recruitment can sometimes take many weeks.

If, however, they have promised to let you know, one way or the other, by a certain date and that day comes and goes, there is no harm done by telephoning to see how soon you are going to find out their decision.

Remember the interviewer is hoping that you are the right person for the job just as you are hoping to get the job. Do prepare and practise. It will be worth it.

Good luck!

ACTIVITY 32

Assessment centres

⮕ Diligence is the mother of good luck.   Benjamin Franklin

Pioneered in the UK by the armed forces, assessment centres are now used by a number of organisations to select junior managers. They are very often re-labelled 'development centres' and used for internal selection purposes to identify fast-trackers and people with potential for promotion. For most candidates it's a once in a lifetime opportunity.

If you're invited to attend an assessment centre the following 'inside information' could be invaluable. See also the Activities on presentation skills, interview skills and tests and evaluations. A form at the end of this Activity summarises the exercises at a typical assessment centre.

INSIDE INFORMATION

- Get as much sleep as you can beforehand. It's highly likely that, just as you're starting to relax, you'll be handed a mammoth task with a tight deadline to see how you respond under pressure.

- Keep your eyes and ears open and observe the performance of the other candidates. You may be asked to rate their performance. Be prepared to give a factual and analytical summary of their contribution.

- Don't be lulled into a false sense of security by thinking the assessors are off-duty, if you've been invited to join everyone for dinner the night before the assessment centre. They will probably be assessing your social competence over dinner, in the bar, over breakfast …

- Even if you haven't been asked to prepare a presentation, brush up on your skills. There is a good chance that you'll be asked to prepare one at short notice: Pre-select two topics: 'an improvement you've made at work' and an 'interesting angle on your hobby'.

- If you're invited to attend an assessment centre in a hotel, a few casual questions to the manager or receptionist may give you a good idea of what's in store. If the assessors have spent the early part of the day setting up a network of computers in syndicate rooms, then it sounds as if you're going to be involved in a computer-based business simulation. Great fun!

- Try to think through the qualities the assessors will be looking for: leadership, interpersonal skills, ability to handle stress, verbal communication, written communication, flexibility, negotiation skills, problem-solving, business skills, commercial acumen, decision-taking, initiative and creativity. Clearly the weightings will change depending on the job, but commercial acumen, interpersonal skills and flexibility must be high on everyone's list.

- Don't try to suppress other candidates in an attempt to make the assessors notice only you. You will come across as overbearing and insensitive.

ASSESSMENT CENTRE EXERCISES

Assessment centres are usually designed to include exercises which will measure you against the aspects of the job. For all of the exercises make sure you understand the chairperson's instructions or the written brief. If you don't, ask!

Not listening and not reading instructions thoroughly are the two biggest causes of frustration in candidates. I have been moaned at and even shouted at by candidates who had not read instructions properly. Having a go at the chairperson is a career-limiting step, I can tell you! Remember, you're being tested!

The following are common exercises.

In-tray exercises

You are given the 'in-tray' of a senior manager and have one hour to 'get through it' – otherwise you'll miss your plane! You'll be asked to write on each item what you would do with it, or write a reply to letters.

- Sort the whole thing first and prioritise every item: A (top priority), B and C. (They have probably 'buried' some important details near the bottom!)

- Start with the As and work your way through.

- Resignations and other 'people' issues are top priority, As.

- Wherever you can, make a note that you would make a telephone call, or send an E-mail – the MD of one of my client companies, says that he writes no more than four memos per year.

- If you do write memos, write key messages and let your 'secretary' compose the letter.

- Familiarise yourself with the organisational structure of the company and the briefing instructions before you start.

Sales or negotiation role play

You are asked to sell a product or negotiate a deal.

- Ask 'probing' questions: How?, Why?, When?, Where?, What? and Which? are best for gathering information.

- Listen to the answers and try to match the needs of the customer with what the product does! To give an example, one of the all-time favourites when recruiting new salespeople is for the interviewer to say, 'OK sell this fountain pen to me'. Unenlightened candidates immediately start prattling on about style, design, gold nibs and good ink flow. The smart ones ask questions like, 'Do you use a fountain pen?', 'What qualities are important to you when you're choosing a new pen?', 'What would you expect to pay for a fountain pen?'. And then go on to match the product's features and benefits to customer needs. People who do badly in these exercises do so because they're too busy putting over their own viewpoint, based on assumptions, rather than asking questions to find out what the 'customer' wants!

Business simulation

This may be paper-based or computer-based.

You are split into small groups and over a series of rounds, compete with other groups to develop, manufacture, market and distribute products Great fun!

- Play to win!

- Invest in research for new products in the early rounds – products don't last forever.

- As you get results back at the end of each round analyse the performance of the competitors – you may be able to undercut them or market your product to a niche.

Group discussion (interactive skills)

You are given a problem to solve as a group. Common problems are simulations where your group have been stranded at sea, in the desert or on the moon. (See page 204 for an example of an assessor's form.)

- If you're 'stranded' in the desert or on the ocean, being detected is the first priority, followed by food – don't move away to try to save yourself; search parties look for your last location!
- Formulate your own ideas quickly and sell them convincingly to the group.
- Suggest that the group needs a structure and timetable to work to; and propose one.
- Don't steamroller other people's ideas, listen attentively.
- If someone isn't contributing, draw them into the group by asking for their ideas.
- Five minutes before the end suggest that you need to summarise your decision and take control of whatever needs to be done.

MAKE THE MOST OF THE OPPORTUNITY

An assessment centre is a tremendous opportunity for you to show what you can do. Prepare yourself well and enjoy it. In summary, be positive, be prepared to play the game and project an image of your real self.

INTERACTIVE SKILLS ASSESSMENT

Candidate name —————————————   Assessor —————————————

Behaviour	Quality/quantity of contribution	Rating
Giving information		
Seeking information		
Supporting others		
Disagreeing with others		
Persuading others		
Controlling others		
Other contributions		

COMMENTS

STANDARDS

5   Much more than acceptable (significantly above criteria required for successful job performance)

4   More than acceptable (generally exceeds criteria relative to quality and quantity of behaviour required)

3   Acceptable (meets criteria relative to quality and quantity of behaviour required)

2   Less than acceptable (generally does not meet criteria relative to quality and quantity of behaviour required)

1   Much less than acceptable (significantly below criteria required for successful job performance)

Overall rating ————————————

SELECTION PANEL ASSESSMENT FORM: POSITION _____

Chairperson _____ Interview date: _____

Other panel members _____

_____

EXERCISE

Candidate	Leaderless group	In-tray exercise	Presentation	Marketing plan	1:1 negotiation	Interpersonal /social skills	Interview no. 1	Interview no. 2	Assessment

Panel recommendation:

ACTIVITY 33

Making a presentation

➡ It usually takes me more than three weeks to prepare a
good impromptu speech.   Mark Twain

To assess your self-confidence, ability to communicate and ability to handle a mini-project, some organisations may ask you to make a short presentation either to a group of managers or, for very senior positions, to the board of directors. Others incorporate a presentation into their assessment centre exercises.

The subject can vary: debating the pros and cons of subjects like E-commerce, mobile comunications and M-commerce, or you may be asked to present a mini-marketing plan for one of the company's products. They may even leave the choice of subject to you. If this happens do not pick 'Where I took my holiday' or 'My hobby'. Do choose a business-related subject that you know something about. The time you are given to prepare can vary from 30 minutes to many days.

If you are asked to give a presentation do take it seriously – management time is very valuable and if the company have gathered an audience to listen to you, then you can be sure that they will be taking it seriously.

Unless you are a natural or are well-experienced, you will probably be nervous. This is a good thing. If you didn't have at least some degree of anxiety then you probably aren't taking the exercise seriously.

The keys to an effective presentation are preparation, planning and practice.

PREPARE THE CONTENT

Most people find knowing where to begin is the most difficult step. If you are one of these people I can guarantee the following steps will help you present confidently.

Ask yourself – 'What do I want the audience to learn from my presentation?'.

Write this objective in the middle of a blank page. Now let your mind 'freewheel' to produce a mind-map of ideas. The mind-map on page 206 is the one I drew when I started to plan this Activity, which was originally published as an article called 'How to give a presentation and live to tell the tale'.

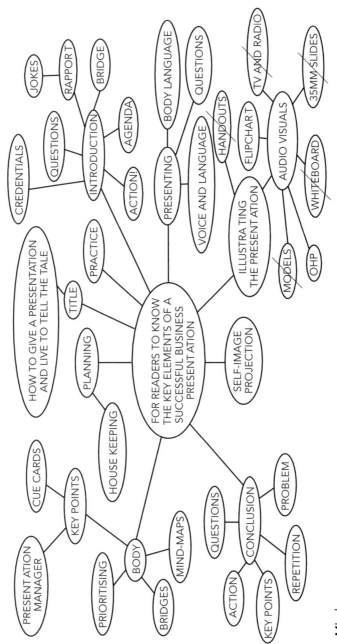

Mind-map

You'll find that you have far too many things to say, so the next step is to edit and give the presentation some structure.

Now choose the most important point which you want to communicate. Write it in on the presentation planner (there is a blank copy at the end of this Activity) as key point No. 1. Now add the others in descending order of priority.

Yes, I know that the natural tendency is to save the best to last, but remember that people are most attentive at the start.

Now develop your content by putting the information from your mind-map into your key points. Remember, only information which is relevant to achieving your objectives is allowed. Limit your key points to a maximum of five. Three is even better. Think about the presenters you admire – are they the ones who put over powerful and succinct argument or are they the people who waffle and constantly overrun?

You have now developed the main body of your presentation. But before we move on, decide how you will link or bridge from one point to the next. A phrase like, 'Now let us look at the introduction' lets the listeners know you've finished one topic and gives a signpost of what's next.

Other useful bridges are: enumerating – 'first …, second …, etc.' when you've stated that you have a specific number of points to cover; 'On the contrary' or 'On the other hand' when you're weighing pros and cons; or simply, 'Next …'. To avoid sounding hackneyed, use a different bridge to move from each of your key points. Now write them on your presentation planner.

Your introduction

You get one opportunity to make a first impression. So how do you create that positive impression from the start?

The first step is to establish empathy by building a bridge to as many audience members as you can. If you can, speak informally to each person before you begin.

When you stand to address the group, reinforce the bridge by saying how much you've been looking forward to meeting them … and pay some compliment to their office, factory, etc.

If you're considering starting with a joke, my advice is don't. You never know whom you may offend and alienate. This isn't to say you shouldn't be warm, friendly and charming. But, as well as having the potential to offend, comedy is the most difficult of all stage techniques to master, as any actor will tell you.

Now say what you're going to talk about, seen from their viewpoint.

But why should they listen to you? You should say a few words here about why you are qualified to speak on this topic, what you have done to research the subject, what is your background in this field, etc. Two or three sentences establish your credibility.

Now for the agenda. Give the audience a 'map' of what you'll be talking about. The agenda is a list of the key points which make up the body of the presentation.

'As we go through the presentation please feel free to ask questions, if I haven't explained anything clearly; although we do have a few moments at the end for questions.' Let's face it, telling people to save their questions until the end rarely works. So why not prepare for it? Doing it this way also signals to the audience that you're confident of what your talking about.

Next, state quite clearly what you want them to do as a result of listening to you; the action request. 'When I've finished speaking I hope you will see that the strategy I am advocating will help to re-position (product) in the market-place.'

And finally your bridge. How do you link to the first key point in the body?

Now write each of these into your presentation planner.

In conclusion

Your conclusion should be short and to the point, but not rushed. You want to encapsulate your presentation into a package that they can take away with them.

Remind them of the problem or opportunity. Restate your key points and crystalise the message. State your request action – what you want them to do?

This structure for your presentation ensures that your key points are repeated at least three times and repetition is a very powerful persuader. Just watch commercial television to see how often advertisements are repeated, if you need convincing.

Now write your conclusion on your presentation planner.

To summarise, with apologies to whoever said it first, your structure will allow you to: 'Tell them what you're going to tell them, then tell them and then tell them what you've told them.'

PLAN YOUR RESOURCES

Now you have decided what you are going to say, you can concentrate on how you say it. Transfer your introduction, key points (in the correct order) and conclusion on to postcards, using single words to act as stab points. Do not write a script, it will make your voice become dull and lifeless.

Now punch a hole into the top right-hand corner of each card and loosely tie them together with a piece of string. This way your presentation will keep in the correct order, even if you drop the cards. (When you deliver your presentation, don't be afraid to glance at your cue cards. A momentary pause is far more acceptable than waffle or a deathly hush, because you can't think what to say next.)

Visual aids are useful in your presentation since they can convey information – try describing in words the layout of a printed circuit board or how to fold a napkin! Your visual aids reinforce what you are saying by focusing the audience's attention.

The most convenient visual aids to use are the flipcharts or overhead transparencies. Either is available at good commercial stationers.

The flipchart can be very useful for developing diagrams in front of your audience – write the words/draw the diagram in advance in pencil on the flipchart sheet. The audience will not be able to see the fine lines and you will be confident that the layout will be correct when you start to build up the chart in front of your audience, using marker pens. Ensure that you have at least two pens available and check that they both work before the presentation.

Overhead transparencies are a convenient way for producing visual aids. Nowadays, you'll be out of the running if you're applying for anything other than the most junior position and you don't use one of the software packages like MS PowerPoint or Lotus Freelance to generate your visuals. You may even be asked to take your presentation visuals on a floppy disk, so that they can be projected using an electronic data projector. If you don't have access to a computer, many high street print-shops can produce your transparencies for you. They can also photocopy diagrams or words directly onto transparencies. In an emergency, or if you really haven't got the money or resources, you can use special pens and handwrite them (I prefer the permanent kind since they do not smudge). Use only dark colours – pretty as the yellows and oranges are, they can't be read!

Whichever visual aids you use, follow the basic principles of keeping them as simple as possible. Use large letters and single words as stab points so that they can be read easily. Do not write complete sentences. Remember a picture is worth a thousand words. As a general rule allow 45 seconds to 1 minute per transparency when planning your time.

PRACTISE

Rehearse your presentation once or twice so that you know what you are going to say and how you are going to say it. Use a friend as a timekeeper to give you constructive feedback.

ANSWERING QUESTIONS

Generally speaking, the assessors are aware of your time pressures and so will save questions until the end.

If you're asked a question that you can't answer then be honest – you'll gain more credibility from this than from half-baked waffle. You can in fact turn your lack of knowledge to your advantage by saying to the questioner: 'That's an interesting point which I haven't been asked before. I'm afraid I don't have an answer for you right now, but I will find out and get back to you.' This technique flatters the questioner's ego and demonstrates your integrity.

PREPARATION AND PRESENTATION

Get a good night's sleep and no matter how nervous you are, avoid alcohol or stimulants!

Here are a few dos and don'ts for you to bear in mind when presenting.

Do	Don't
Use global vision to include everyone	Use non-words, like ums and errs
Hold eye contact with people	Jingle coins/keys in pockets
Check focus beforehand	Clean out/scratch orifices
Check power beforehand	Talk to the floor, the screen or one main audience member
Set up the room beforehand	Read visuals word for word
Use clear, concise visuals	Joke – you don't know whom you might offend
Vary tone and speed of your voice	Mumble
Stand relatively stationary	Apologise for what you're going to say
Have spare pens/transparencies	Dress outrageously
Keep to time	Smoke – even if audience members do
Use simple language	Remove your jacket
End on a positive note	Use a pointer – they're too easy to play with

WHAT ARE THE ASSESSORS LOOKING FOR?

Unless you've applied for a job as a television presenter or a similar position which involves speaking to groups on a regular basis, it is unlikely that the assessors will be looking for outstanding skills.

The assessors will be looking for you to communicate your message effectively, for you to project yourself confidently and for you to know what you are talking about. They'll also be trying to gauge how much work you have put into the exercise and how seriously you took it. I once ran an assessment centre where the two of the candidates were 'late entries'. Each of them received the briefing pack the day before. One candidate gave a very poor talk from some scribbled notes and apologised, making the excuse that she hadn't had time to prepare. The other candidate gave an excellent presentation, with professionally produced transparencies, and hand-outs of her talk for the assessors. She made no mention of the short amount of time she'd had to prepare. Let me ask, who do you think made the best impression? And, everything else being equal, who would you have employed?

Finally. Remember, even the most experienced presenters get nervous – use the adrenaline to help you to excel!

The form on the next page is an example of what may be used to assess your presentation.

ASSESSMENT CENTRE – PRESENTATION SCORE SHEET

Candidate name ———————————— Assessor ——————————

Ten-minute presentation with five-minutes questions and answers from assessors.

Criteria	Comments	Rating
Content		
Delivery (voice/posture)		
Pace		
Use of visuals		
Audience contact		
Handling questions		
Other comments		

STANDARDS

5 Much more than acceptable (significantly above criteria required for successful job performance)

4 More than acceptable (generally exceeds criteria relative to quality and quantity of behaviour required)

3 Acceptable (meets criteria relative to quality and quantity of behaviour required)

2 Less than acceptable (generally does not meet criteria relative to quality and quantity of behaviour required)

1 Much less than acceptable (significantly below criteria required for successful job performance)

Overall rating _____

PRESENTATION PLANNER

Introduction	Main body	Conclusion
Rapport statement	Key point 1	Remind them of the problem/opportunity
Presentation subject	Bridge	
Your credentials	Key point 2	Restate the key points and crystallise the message
Agenda	Bridge	
Question request	Key point 3	
	Bridge	
Action request	Key point 4	Request action
	Bridge	
Bridge	Key point 5	
	Bridge	

ACTIVITY (34)

Tests and evaluations

⟹ It is hard to fail, but it is worse never to have tried to succeed. In this life we get nothing save by effort.   Theodore Roosevelt

Some organisations use tests and evaluations in their selection process.

Before inviting people to interview, the recruiter identifies personality traits, skills and knowledge which would be held by the ideal candidate. During the selection process candidates are asked to complete 'tests' to evaluate whether they possess these qualities.

The extent of the testing can vary from a short five-minute form-filling exercise through to a whole day, involving a battery of tests and evaluations and an interview with a psychologist.

I cannot stress too strongly that there is no need to get anxious about the tests! I know it's easy for me to say that ... I'm not the one who has been invited to interview! Seriously, the tests will not reveal that really you're an alien from Mars (you aren't, are you?) or that you're not really a person ... you're a slug who lives in an aquarium and just for today you've transformed yourself into a person! Take them in your stride do your best and be honest.

You should also read the appendices Internet Recruitment, Our Ally (page 239) and Psychometric Testing (page 242). These articles have been contributed by SHL and ASE respectively. Between them, these two companies provide psychometric assessment and consulting services to over 6000 organisations and so their advice is well worth taking!

PERSONALITY QUESTIONNAIRES

As their name implies the questionnaires aim to gain an insight into your personality. I do not like the use of the word 'test' when related to personality evaluations. 'Test' implies 'right and wrong' and in personality evaluations there are no right and wrong answers – we are all different.

Usually there is no time limit for a personality questionnaire, but you are advised not to over-analyse your reply and to move quickly from question to question. Don't answer questions as you think you should. Be honest to yourself, otherwise you're defeating the object. Also, some personality questionnaires have an 'in-built' evaluation which checks to see how (honest) consistent your answers have been.

The most commonly used personality questionnaires are the Myers-Briggs Type Inventory (MBTI) that claims to be the most widely used one in the world; the SHL Occupational Personality Quotient (SHL OPQ); the Sixteen Personality Factors (16PF); and one by Thomas International. There are many others.

SKILLS AND APTITUDE TESTS

Unlike personality questionnaires, skill and aptitude tests are designed to test you against standards.

Typing tests are used to evaluate your keyboard skills and typing accuracy. Tests of manual dexterity, such as rebuilding a broken-down model, test your 'motor skills'.

Others represent an intellectual challenge such as numerical, verbal and abstract reasoning tests!

- **Numerical** – Identifies the ability to pick out and manipulate key information from tables, graphs and semi-technical reports.
- **Verbal** – Identifies the ability to pick out information from reports and then make objective decisions based on the information in the text.
- **Abstract** – Tests the ability to think flexibly. The test measures the ability to recognise order in the midst of apparent chaos, to focus on certain aspects of a task and to ignore irrelevant detail.

Your score in the tests will be compared against 'norm' tables to see how you have performed, compared with previous groups of people who have taken the test.

On the following pages are 'test taker's guides'.

The 'general ability tests' are used for the selection of staff below graduate level and for the identification of potential for supervisory and junior management posts, regardless of previous experience or education.

The 'graduate and managerial assessment' tests are used in recruiting at graduate and managerial level.

(I am grateful to ASE, of Windsor, for their permission to reproduce the 'test taker's guides'.)

GENERAL ABILITY TESTS

A TEST TAKER'S GUIDE

You have been sent this leaflet to help you prepare for your testing session. It:

* introduces you to the tests themselves;

* gives you an idea of what to expect;

* provides hints on how to prepare yourself;

* answers key questions; but remember that you can still ask questions at the testing session.

Here are the answers to some important questions.

Q   Why am I being asked to take some tests?

A   You may have school or work qualifications, but these tests give extra information which will help employers to select those applicants who are best suited to the job or their training programme.

Tests also help you to explore your abilities; this should assist you in choosing a suitable area of work.

People who are successful in the job have usually done well in the tests, so both employers and applicants get what they want.

Q   How do they work?

A   Employers decide which skills and abilities are needed in the job. Tests are then selected to measure some of these.

There is a practice period in the testing session to make sure everyone understands how to do the test(s).

The tests are carefully timed, so you may not finish; but you should work as fast as you can and follow the instructions given.

Your answers are then scored and this information is used to help decide whether you will be suitable for the job.

Q   Will I be asked to do anything else?

A   Usually you will be asked to fill in an application form and this information is also very important.

You may also be interviewed. Employers use information from many sources to help them make the best decision.

THE TEST SESSION

When you come to the session you will be asked to do the tests ticked below. The time shown beside each test is the time you will be allowed once you have been given the introductory examples and practice test. Remember you will be given a break between the tests.

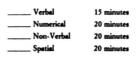

_____	**Verbal**	**15 minutes**
_____	**Numerical**	**20 minutes**
_____	**Non-Verbal**	**20 minutes**
_____	**Spatial**	**20 minutes**

Look at the examples given for each of the tests you will be taking. None of these examples will be in the real tests.

Check that you understand the questions and correct answers. Remember that if you do not understand there will be time to ask before the test begins.

THE ANSWER SHEET

You will be given a separate answer sheet for each test. The one given below is from the Verbal Test and is marked with the correct answers for the examples given. The Numerical and Non-Verbal answer sheets are very similar.

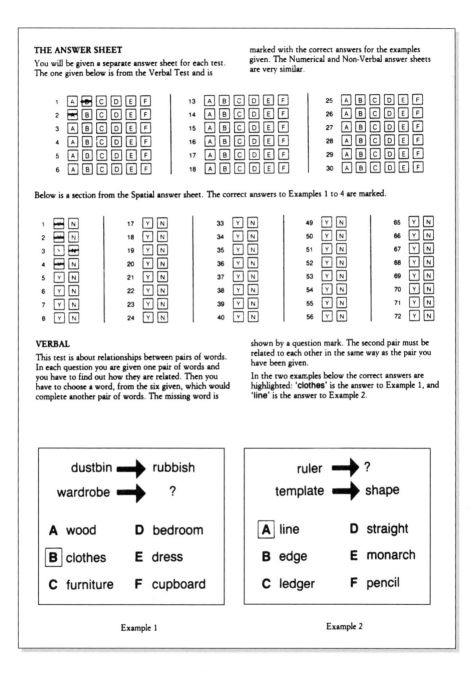

Below is a section from the Spatial answer sheet. The correct answers to Examples 1 to 4 are marked.

VERBAL

This test is about relationships between pairs of words. In each question you are given one pair of words and you have to find out how they are related. Then you have to choose a word, from the six given, which would complete another pair of words. The missing word is shown by a question mark. The second pair must be related to each other in the same way as the pair you have been given.

In the two examples below the correct answers are highlighted: 'clothes' is the answer to Example 1, and 'line' is the answer to Example 2.

dustbin ➡ rubbish

wardrobe ➡ ?

A wood   D bedroom

B clothes   E dress

C furniture   F cupboard

Example 1

ruler ➡ ?

template ➡ shape

A line   D straight

B edge   E monarch

C ledger   F pencil

Example 2

NON-VERBAL

In this test you have to work out relationships between shapes. There are two basic types of question. In the first, as Example 1, you are given two large figures inside an oval. You have to decide how they are alike, which may be in one way or several ways. Only one figure at the bottom also has all these qualities. In this case there is a small shape followed by a dotted line, then two solid lines. Only figure A fits this description. The correct answer has been highlighted.

In the other questions, such as Examples 2 and 3, there is a grid which contains an arrangement of shapes with one missing section. This is marked by the question mark. You have to decide how the shapes are related to each other and decide which of the six possibilities is the missing one.

In Example 2, the three figures in the centre of each big triangle are repeated in the outer triangles next to them. Also, each repeated figure has either a circle or a triangle around it. Here, the answer is 'F'.

In Example 3, a different grid is used. The answer, which is 'A', can be found by looking at the pattern of shapes in the inside and outside triangles.

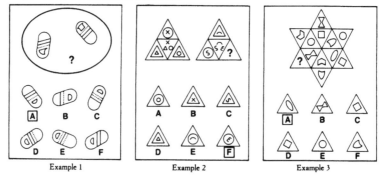

Example 1   Example 2   Example 3

NUMERICAL

In this test you have to work out the relationship between numbers. All questions have an arrangement of numbers in a grid with one or two numbers missing. The missing numbers are shown by question marks. You have to find how the numbers are related to each other and so decide which of the six possibilities is the missing one.

If you look at the first example below, the numbers in the 'chain' on the left-hand side go in sequence by 'doubling up'. Thus, twice 3 is 6; twice 6 is 12; and twice 12 is 24. Therefore the missing answer is 24 or 'C'. The correct answer has been highlighted.

Sometimes you have two numbers missing and you will have to find the answer which has them both. In Example 2 you have to look across the rows and down the columns rather like a crossword. Going across the rows, the numbers increase by the same amount; going down the rows they double each time. You must find the two numbers that fit both of these rules. The missing numbers are 14 and 20, which is answer 'A'.

In Example 3, you again must find the two missing numbers. Here, the bottom number on the left is always 21 more than the top number, and the one on the right is always 10 more than the top numbers. Thus, the correct answer is 'A'.

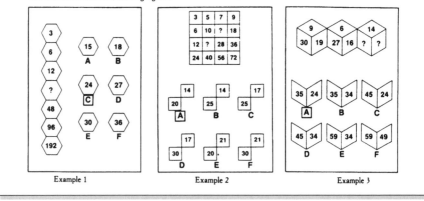

Example 1   Example 2   Example 3

SPATIAL

In this test you have to imagine what a flat pattern would look like if it were cut out and folded into a solid object. The patterns have to be folded along the black lines so that the markings are on the outside of the solid object.

You have to decide if each of the solid objects shown below the flat pattern could be made from it when folded. Answer 'no' if an object definitely **could not** be made and 'yes' if it definitely **could** be made. If you cannot be sure without seeing the hidden side, answer 'yes'.

In Example 1, if the pattern were folded it would form a long shape with one black side and the dot in the middle on one of the ends. Question 1 clearly could be this shape with the black side and dot in the correct places. Similarly, the answer to question 2 is 'yes' since there is one black side and you can only see one of the ends; the other one could have the dot on it. However, the answer to question 3 is clearly 'no' since the long side on the top left should be black. Question 4 is 'yes' because the black side is hidden under the shape. The correct answers are under the questions.

In Example 2 the answers to questions 5, 6 and 7 are 'yes', while the answer to 8 is 'no'.

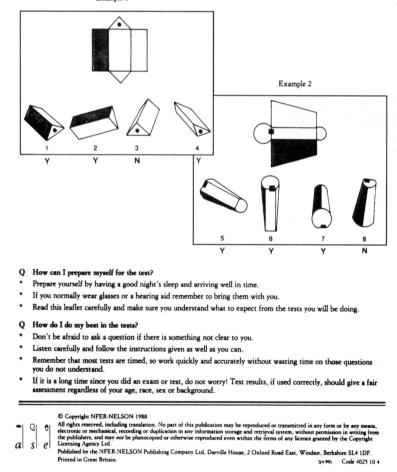

Example 1

Example 2

Q How can I prepare myself for the test?

* Prepare yourself by having a good night's sleep and arriving well in time.
* If you normally wear glasses or a hearing aid remember to bring them with you.
* Read this leaflet carefully and make sure you understand what to expect from the tests you will be doing.

Q How do I do my best in the tests?

* Don't be afraid to ask a question if there is something not clear to you.
* Listen carefully and follow the instructions given as well as you can.
* Remember that most tests are timed, so work quickly and accurately without wasting time on those questions you do not understand.
* If it is a long time since you did an exam or test, do not worry! Test results, if used correctly, should give a fair assessment regardless of your age, race, sex or background.

GRADUATE AND MANAGERIAL ASSESSMENT

A Test Taker's Guide

Part of our organization's selection system involves the use of tests. The reason for using tests is simply to collect as much information as possible about each person to help us make a more informed and fairer decision.

You have been sent this leaflet to help you prepare for your testing session. It has been designed to:

- introduce you to the tests themselves;
- give you an idea of what to expect;
- provide hints on how to prepare yourself;
- answer key questions; but remember that you can still ask questions at the testing session.

Here are the answers to some important questions.

Q   Why am I being asked to take some tests?

A   You may have work, training or vocational qualifications, but these tests give extra information which will help us to select people who are best suited to the job or who will benefit from a development or training programme. People who are successful in the job tend to do well in the tests, so everybody gets what they want.

Q   How do they work?

A   We have found out which skills and abilities are needed in the job. We then chose tests to measure some of these skills and abilities.

There is a practise period in each test to make sure everyone understands how to do it. Remember you can ask questions during the practice period. The tests are carefully timed, and you probably will not finish; but remember to work as fast as you can and follow the instructions given. Do not spend too long on any one question. Toward the end of each test, review your answers and the questions you have not answered. At this stage, even if you are not absolutely sure of an answer, make it anyway. There is no penalty for guessing and any answer is better than none at all.

When the test is over your answers will be scored and this information will be used to help decide whether you will be suitable for the job or training programme.

Q   Will I be asked to do anything else?

A   You may be interviewed or asked to take part in practical exercises or group activities. We use information from as many sources as possible to help us make the best decision.

The Test Session

When you come to the session you will be asked to do one or more of the tests ticked below. The time shown beside each test is the time you will be allowed after you have been given the introductory examples and practise test. Remember you will be given a break between the tests.

	Abstract	30 minutes
	Verbal	30 minutes
	Numerical	30 minutes

·Look at the examples overleaf for each of the tests you will be taking. None of these examples will be in the real tests. Check that you understand the questions and correct answers. Reading them more than once may help you understand them. Remember that if you have questions there will be time to ask before the test begins.

The Answer Sheet

You will be given a separate answer sheet for each test. Here is part of the abstract answer sheet. It is marked with the correct answers for the examples given below. The Verbal and Numerical answer sheets are very similar.

1 ⬥ IB IC.
2 IA ⬥ IC
3 IA' IB' ⬥ '
4 IA' IB ⬥
5 ⬥ IB IC'

6 IA' IB' ICI
7 IA' IB' ICI
8 IA IB IC
9 IA IB IC'
10 IA IB IC.

Abstract

This is a test of your skill at finding similarities and differences in groups of patterns. Each item consists of three sets of patterns. There are two groups of four, one marked A and another marked B, and a set of five separate patterns which are numbered.

All the patterns in Group A are in some way similar to each other, and all those in Group B are similar to each other. However, the two groups are different, and you should be able to identify the basis for this difference by studying them.

When you have worked out why the patterns in Groups A and B are grouped as they are, you should then decide to which group each of the five separately numbered patterns belongs.

If you decide that a pattern belongs to Group A, put a line through A next to that pattern's number on the answer sheet. Similarly, if you decide that a pattern belongs to Group B, put a line through B. If you decide that a pattern belongs to neither Group A nor Group B then put a line through C on the answer sheet.

Incidentally, the patterns in the A and B groups are in no particular arrangement or order, so don't waste time looking for sequences amongst the groups of four, or matches between patterns in the A and B Groups in corresponding positions.

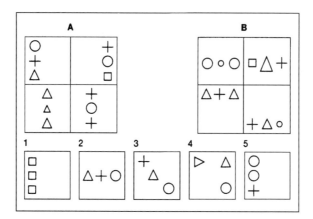

In the example above, each pattern in Group A consists of shapes arranged vertically; and each of the Group B patterns consist of shapes arranged horizontally. So patterns 1 and 5 belong with Group A, pattern 2 belongs with Group B and patterns 3 and 4 do not belong to either, so they are in Group C.

Verbal

This is a test of your skill at making sense of reports which cannot be relied upon to be objective, truthful or even consistent.

The test consists of a series of short passages of prose, each of which includes a number of statements intended to convey information, or persuade the reader of a point of view.

Each passage is accompanied by four statements relating to the information or arguments it contains. Assume that what is stated in the passage is true – even if it contradicts what you know or believe to be the case in reality – and decide for each statement whether, on this assumption, it is true or false, or whether you cannot tell and need more information.

The definitions are:

True: This means that the statement is already made in the passage, that it is implied by, or follows logically from a statement or statements made in the passage.

False: This means that the statement contradicts a statement made in, implied by, or following logically from, the passage.

Can't tell: This means that there is insufficient information in the passage to draw firm conclusions about the truth or falsity of the statement.

In recent years it has become clear that man's use of fossil fuels is likely to have a major impact on the world's climate. As a result of this, increased concentrations of 'greenhouse' gases such as carbon dioxide and methane will lead to global warming – an overall small increase in average temperatures – whose impact is difficult to predict. Whilst some scientists predict melting of the polar icecaps, and so a rise in sea levels, others think this will be balanced by increased precipitation at the poles.

---

1 | If we go on using fossil fuels at the present rate, we must expect climatic change.

2 | Depletion of the ozone layer will result in global warming.

3 | Scientists are agreed that use of fossil fuels will eventually lead to a rise in sea levels.

4 | The burning of fossil fuels increases the concentration of methane in the atmosphere.

A True   **B False**   **C Can't tell**

In the example above, the answers to 1 and 4 are 'A'. The statements are true on the basis of the information given in the first two sentences of the passage. The answer to 2 is 'C'. No information about the ozone layer is given in the passage so it is impossible to tell whether the statement is true or false. The answer to 3 is 'B'. The statement is false because it contradicts the information given in the last sentence of the passage.

Numerical

This is a test of your skill at reasoning with numbers. First, you are given some information in a variety of forms – text, tables or graphs – followed by three related questions. For each question, choose what you think is the correct answer from the possible answers A to P.

An insurance scheme pays benefits to its members who are sick for extended periods of time at the following rates:

1st month:	nil
2nd – 4th months:	50% of normal salary
5th and succeeding months:	25% of normal salary

on the first £24,000 p.a. of salary for each month in which the member is sick and is not paid by the employer. How much does the scheme pay to:

1 John, who is off work for two months, whose salary is £12,000 p.a., and who gets no sick pay.

2 Pat, who is ill for 6 months, but who is paid normally for the first two months and whose salary is £18,000 p.a..

3 Hilary, whose salary is £30,000 p.a., who gets 3 months' sick pay from her employer, and who has to take 9 months off.

A	£250	B	£500	C	£750	D	£1000
E	£1125	F	£1500	G	£1765	H	£2125
I	£2250	J	£2350	K	£2500	L	£3125
M	£3750	N	£4000	O	£5000	P	£5625

In the example above the answer to 1 is 'B'. The answer to 2 is 'I'. The answer to 3 is 'N'. Remember that, in this example, the scheme operates 'for each month in which the member is sick and is not paid by the employer'. So the scheme only comes into effect once the employer's sick pay stops. Careful reading of the information given will help you answer the questions correctly.

Q How can I prepare myself for the tests?

■ Prepare yourself by having a good night's sleep and arriving well in time.
■ If you normally wear glasses or a hearing aid remember to bring them with you.
■ Read this leaflet carefully and make sure you understand what to expect from the tests you will be doing.

Q How do I do my best in the tests?

■ Don't be afraid to ask a question if there is something not clear to you.
■ Listen carefully and follow the instructions given as well as you can.
■ Remember that most tests are timed, so try to work quickly and accurately.
■ If it is a long time since you did an exam or test, do not worry! Test results, if used correctly, should give a fair assessment regardless of your age, race, sex or background.

a s e

Published by The NFER–NELSON Publishing Company Ltd., Darville House, 2 Oxford Road East, Windsor, Berkshire, SL4 1DF, England.
© 1992, S.F. Blinkhorn
All rights reserved.
Code 4700 14 4

TEAM TYPE QUESTIONNAIRES

Work by Dr Meredith Belbin has shown that groups are most productive when there is a good mixture of people who can contribute various skills to the team. The 'team/type' questionnaire is used to gauge how well you will fit into the team.

None of the team types is the 'best' type to be – productive teams have a mix of the different types.

The following summary describes the various team types:

- **Plant:** Creative, imaginative, unorthodox. Solves difficult problems. Weak in communicating with and managing ordinary people.

- **Resource investigator:** Extrovert, enthusiastic, communicative. Explores opportunities. Develops contacts. Loses interest once initial enthusiasm has passed.

- **Chairperson/co-ordinator:** Mature, confident and trusting. A good chairperson clarifies goals, promotes decision-making. Not necessarily the most clever or creative member of a group.

- **Shaper:** Dynamic, outgoing, highly strung. Challenges, pressurises, finds ways round obstacles. Prone to provocation and short-lived bursts of temper.

- **Monitor evaluator:** Sober, strategic and discerning. Sees all options. Judges accurately. Lacks drive and ability to inspire others.

- **Teamworker:** Social, mild, perceptive and accommodating. Listens, builds, averts friction. Indecisive in crunch situations.

- **Company worker/implementer:** Disciplined, reliable, conservative and efficient. Turns ideas into practical actions. Somewhat inflexible, slow to respond to new possibilities.

- **Completer:** Painstaking, conscientious, anxious. Searches out errors and omissions. Delivers on time. Inclined to worry unduly. Reluctant to delegate.

- **Expert/specialist:** Single-minded, self-starting, dedicated. Provides knowledge or technical skills in rare supply. Contributes only on a narrow front.

To find out your own 'team type' you'll need Dr Belbin's book, *Management Teams: Why They Succeed or Fail*, which contains the questionnaire.

DRUG AND ALCOHOL TESTING

Concerned with the effect that alcohol and drug abuse has on productivity, some employers require a urine sample which is tested for drugs and alcohol. These tests are very rare in the UK but common in the USA, so they are more likely if you're applying to the UK affiliate of a large US company.

GRAPHOANALYSIS (HANDWRITING ANALYSIS)

You won't even be aware that it's being carried out! Graphoanalysis claims to be able to interpret the personality of a person from their handwriting. It is widely used, I understand, in continental Europe, particularly in France, but is not in the UK, although one UK consultancy offering this service has over 100 clients.

FEEDBACK

To end on a positive note! A good employer will always give you feedback from these tests, whether you get offered the job or not – but usually only if you ask!

Profiling instruments, evaluations, assessments, or whatever you wish to call them, are not free: they cost the recruiting organisation both time and money. If they're being used, they're serious about your application.

They are another way for you to show you're the right person for the job!

ACTIVITY (35)

What if I didn't get the job I wanted?

⟹ Every noble work is at first impossible.   Thomas Carlyle

You were down to a shortlist of two. People were making such positive noises about how you would fit into the organisation and then a letter this morning … 'Thank you for attending interview … I am sorry to inform you that …' and the world falls away from under your feet.

CAN YOU TURN THE SITUATION TO ADVANTAGE?

- Write to them quickly to say how disappointed you were and how impressed you had been with their company. Say that if any other vacancies arise in the near future you would like to be considered. Alternatively, telephone them to say the same things and to ask for some feedback on why you didn't get the job – most employers will give you some constructive critique and you never know, you may be able to re-open discussions; it can work. (See Activity 28.)

- Follow up your letter with a phone call.

- What have you learned from the process? It may be not to put all your eggs in one basket or to conduct yourself differently at recruitment interviews.

Make a few notes below.

Lessons learned from unsuccessful jobsearches

_____

_____

_____

ACTIVITY 36

What if I did get the job I wanted?

➡ Experience shows us that success is due less to ability than to zeal. The winner is the one who gives themselves to their work; body and soul.   Charles Buxton

Congratulate yourself!

CELEBRATE!

And don't forget to say thank you to those who have helped you on your way. Well done.

'Yippee, I got the new job!' (candidate's view). 'Yippee I've filled the vacancy!' (employer's view). 'I think it's what's called a win-win scenario by negotiators. Both parties have benefited.

As soon as your potential employer starts to display buying signals you should be ready to begin the negotiation around your earnings package.

I've said earlier that you should let the employer raise salary first, but you should also realise that they will not normally make their best offer up-front.

Yippee – I've filled the vancancy!'   'Yippee – I got the job.'

NEGOTIATING THE BEST PACKAGE

What we obtain too cheap, we esteem too lightly; it is dearness only that gives everything its value.   Thomas Paine

In some occupations, salaries are fixed according to seniority and years of
service. In others there is a good deal of flexibility around certain variables.

Remember, when you have accepted an offer, you have accepted it. You'll create
a bad impression if you accept the job and then go back two days later, trying to
re-negotiate the terms of the contract.

So before you enter the negotiating arena it's worth working out what is the
minimum package you are prepared to accept and what you would like to get.

Realistically, there will be some aspects of the package which will be fixed, e.g.
holidays, and which will be written in policies and procedures.

KNOWLEDGE IS POWER

The table on page 232 is taken from a real salary survey,* with the job title
removed for confidentiality. The absolute numbers are irrelevant, but the range is
very important. As you will see, there are large differences between the minimum
and maximum salaries and values of company cars. The lowest paid job pays
£17,000 p.a. with no company car while the best job pays almost £32,000 p.a.
with a £15,000 company car. A huge difference, yet these people hold the same
job title, in different organisations.

While you are in the discussing phase, i.e. before anything is committed to paper, ask:

1   Where does the salary fit into their own internal salary scales?

2   Where does the salary fit in, on the salary surveys, for a person with similar
    experience doing a similar job? Company policy may be that they pay a 'lower
    quartile' salary (in other words 75 per cent of people doing a similar job earn more)
    to a new starter, with the objective of shifting you to the upper quartile within
    three years. Try to convince them that your skills and experience warrant being
    started higher up the scale.

Don't be greedy, but do be thorough. Many of the employment agency websites contain salary calculators and advice.

Remember, you probably won't be able to re-negotiate a package once you have accepted it so tread carefully.

An extra £500 per year over a career is an awful lot of money!

(*Salary survey example kindly supplied by Alan Jones & Associates.)

A SURVEY GROUP

JOB 88: CONFIDENTIAL

JOB SALARY DETAILS

ALAN JONES & ASSOCIATES   A.J

TOTAL NUMBER OF JOBHOLDERS : 70
NO. OF COMPANIES REPORTING : 19

COMPANY CODE(L)	JOB HLDRS	MOD RATE MNTH	SALARY MINIMUM	SALARY CONTROL	SALARY MAXIMUM	AVG BASIC	AVG BonusF	AVG BonusV	AVG TOTAL	AVG COMPA RATIO	MED BASIC	MED BonusV	MED BonusF	MED TOTAL	MED COMPA RATIO	CAR VALUE
01 (2)	1	5	25142	31428	37713	31250		601	31851	99	31250	601		31851	99	15184
28 (3)	2	17	19425	26574	33900	23261	447	4280	27988	88	23361	4280	447	27988	88	13655
10 (3)	1	17	24549	30066	35410	26586	1108		27694	88	26586		1108	27694	88	17050
18 (2)	1	1	23606	29508	35814	26000			26000	95	26000			26000	95	14000
22 (4)	8	1	19945	24170	29385	24475		1244	25719	101	23599	1200		24200	81	13000
07 (3)	4	3	23300	25227	34949	24590		726	25316	81	24365	726		25316	87	0
19 (4)	1	8	20182	25227	30272	24882			24882	99	23100			24365	100	17040
02 (4)	6	11	22300	27870	33440	23440		808	24570	100	23238	808	662	23585	83	15300
16 (3)	2	1	19731	24664	29996	23440	880		24320	84	21704	347		23657	88	11500
17 (4)	4	12	21122	26454	31785	21704		1953	23657	88	22000	1953		23845	83	14334
11 (4)	12	1	20097	25122	30146	21763		1750	23513	82	22250	1845		22250	93	13634
24 (4)	3	1	16888	20859	26030	22713			22713	93	22250			21460	94	0
15 (4)	4	1	17562	21952	26342	19502		567	21627	90	20502	567	1558	21460	93	15000
23 (4)	4	10	18000	19842	26069	20650		810	21460	94	20650	810		21450	98	0
05 (4)	7	8	18600	22840	27005	19050			19805	98	19850			19825	100	12700
20 (4)	6	7	18900		21500	18900		900	19800	93	19125	695		18300	84	0
12 (4)	3	0	12819	14594	16282	17000			17000	116	18300			17000	92	11389

	SALARY RANGE CONTROL UNWTD	SALARY RANGE CONTROL WTD	ACTUAL AVERAGE BASIC UNWTD	ACTUAL AVERAGE BASIC WTD	ACTUAL AVERAGE TOTAL UNWTD	ACTUAL AVERAGE TOTAL WTD	ACTUAL MEDIAN BASIC UNWTD	ACTUAL MEDIAN BASIC WTD	ACTUAL MEDIAN TOTAL UNWTD	ACTUAL MEDIAN TOTAL WTD	CAR VALUE UNWTD
MAXIMUM	31428	31428	31250	31250	31851	31851	31250	31250	31851	31851	17050
UPPER QUARTILE	27222	25227	24037	23440	25517	23657	23430	23075	24943	24200	15138
MEDIAN	24664	24417	22713	22713	22713	22713	22250	22250	23657	22250	13827
AVERAGE	24476	23947	22557	21974	23572	21355	22424	21687	23403	22379	14093
LOWER QUARTILE	21838	21952	20262	19875	21355	19875	20262	19875	21355	19875	13125
MINIMUM	14594	14594	17000	17000	17000	17000	17000	17000	17000	17000	11389

ACTIVITY 37

Saying goodbye to my previous employer

➡ Don't flatter yourself that friendship authorises you to say disagreeable things to your intimates. The nearer you come into relation with a person, the more necessary do tact and courtesy become. Oliver Wendell Holmes

THE PRACTICAL ASPECTS

Make sure you know the name of the pension fund administrator so that you can keep them updated of changes of address and whether you want to change pension schemes.

THE PERSONAL ASPECTS

If you're leaving on bad terms DON'T, DON'T, DON'T be rude, abusive or disrespectful to your ex-employer. No matter how much venom there is on the inside, control it and keep it there.

Now, I'm not offering this advice in the interests of your ex-employers, but in yours. No matter how bitter you are feeling, try to leave on amicable terms. The reason for this is that most new employers will want a reference from your past employer. Even if you don't need it immediately for a new job, you might need it in a year or two.

You'll do neither your own self-esteem, nor your future job prospects, any good if you lose your temper and are abusive to your boss. If you want to vent your anger try writing a letter to your ex-boss. Don't hold anything back. Now tear it up and throw it in the waste bin!

Try to 'negotiate' the wording of your reference before you leave so that it can be placed on your personnel file. People move on and it may be that, only a few months after you have left an organisation, a personnel officer whom you have never met will complete a 'company reference' for you, based on the contents of your personnel file.

Tips on how to write your letter of resignation at www.i-resign.com.

ACTIVITY (38)

Starting my new job

⇒ Ah, but a man's reach should exceed his grasp, Or what's heaven for?   Robert Browning

Congratulations. What you have reached for has come within your grasp! Everything we have been working on together has come to fruition.

If I can offer some final advice, don't hide this book away in a cupboard and forget about it – come back to it now and again to see how well you are progressing against your goals.

And don't forget what we have been saying all along about transferable skills – in your jobsearch you have been developing a wide variety of transferable skills: active listening, interpersonal communication and networking to name just three. Transfer them with you into your new job – don't leave them in the cupboard.

ACTIVITY 39

Keeping my new job

New kid on the block

➡ Success is a journey, not a destination. Anon

You get only one opportunity to create a first impression. So, in no order of priority, here are a few things to think about. I hope they will help you to take the right first steps on your new journey.

1 You can choose a lot of things in life, but you can't choose your family and you can't choose your boss! Work on building a good relationship. Identify his/her working style and standards. Find out what's important to them.

2 Create the right first impression. Whether through punctuality, dress or the quality of your work. You're being watched, and labels are applied very quickly and last for a long time. I was nicknamed 'smiler' (ah well, could have been worse) at the age of 11 and am still known by that name to some of my friends! And 'do unto others …' It's what I call the difference between personal power and positional power. People who rely on positional power expect others to click their heels and come running, just because they're the group chief accountant or because they're a supervisor. People with personal power get things done because of their respect for others and their ability to treat them decently.

3 Set the standards. If you're unhappy with the quality of people's work then address it quickly and tactfully. If you're pleased with people's work then say so. Everyone likes praise!

4 Identify and make friends with Taffy and John. Taffy and John were the head of security and the maintenance man at the last company where I worked. They had the finger on the pulse of everything that was going on in the building, and could sort anything from a broken-down car to a hotel booking. I swear that if I'd needed to charter a 747, one of them would have been able to arrange it, and if they couldn't they would have known a 'man who can'!

5   Read your job description and understand what's expected of you. If you haven't got one, ask for one or better still, offer to write it!

6   Ask your boss for feedback. 'How am I doing'?

7   If you don't have an induction programme, ask for one. If there isn't one, then design it yourself, so that in the first month you'll make contact with everyone whom you'll interact with during the course of your work. Which do you think is better for building productive relationships: sitting in an ivory tower and exchanging E-mails with someone you have never met or telephoning, say the production manager, and asking 'I'm new to this industry, could someone show me the production line, so that I can see exactly how we make our products?'

8   Don't be a shirker. Accept new challenges with enthusiasm. Clock-watchers, 9–5ers and those who shy away from work have a short 'shelf life'.

9   Don't keep going on about how wonderful things were at your last company. By all means bring in new ideas, but don't become a CD stuck in replay mode.

10 If you're going to make changes, think through how you're going to communicate the changes, how you're going to implement them, and what the impact on others will be. How will you handle their reaction?

Transformational changes (we were travelling north, we did a handbrake turn and now we're going south west!) tend to ruffle more feathers than incremental changes (if we turn the wheel gently then …). There's a place for both kinds of change, but for both: think it through, then follow through.

Good luck in your new job.
I wish you every success.

When you win … nothing hurts.

Joe Nameth, New York Jets

APPENDIX I

TheJobSearchersSuperstore.com

Visit our website. The website of *3 easy steps to the job you want* is www.TheJob-SearchersSuperstore.com and is dedicated to helping you in your jobsearch.

As this book was going to press, the Annual Recruitment Industry Survey, undertaken by the Recruitment and Employment Federation identified somewhere in the region of 4700 recruitment sites, now available on the Web, and the number is growing daily! How can jobsearchers ever be expected to find their way around this maze of sites?

That's why we have launched the website of this book. At www.TheJob-SearchersSuperstore.com, you'll find independent advice and up-to-date information. You'll also find links to recruitment sites, top employers, as well as lots of career-based sites.

You may wish to make www.TheJobSearchersSuperstore.com your home page, or at least add it to your list of favourites. That way you'll be able to explore different sites, without getting lost in the maze!

If you're eager to get started here are ten good quality sites. But don't forget to pay us a visit (prefix all addresses with www.):

bigbluedog.com   The (London) *Evening Standard's* jobsite.
bt.com/getstarted   Tips on starting your own business.
business-minds.com/gradcareers   FT/Prentice Hall's excellent site for graduates.
careersolutions.co.uk   Careers advice, books and software.
gisajob.com   Jobs and links to employment agencies.
jobsearch.co.uk   Scans your CV and target job and searches for you.
jobsite.co.uk   A site from UK and European recruitment agencies.
monster.co.uk   Leading site; jobs, advice and newsgroups.
stepstone.co.uk   UK and European, job vacancies in many sectors.
wideeyes.co.uk   UK site and jobs worldwide, with free psychometric profile.

Help us to keep www.TheJobSearchersSuperstore.com up-to-date.

With an estimated 10,000 new sites being launched onto the Net each day, we need your help. Please contact us:

- If any of these sites cease to exist.
- If any of the sites that we recommend are carrying out unethical practices.
- If you find a new site for jobsearchers.
- If you own a site for jobsearchers.

E-mail details to: webwatch@TheJobsSearchersSuperstore.com

APPENDIX II

SHL Internet recruitment, our ally

Roy Davis, Head of Communications, SHL

Looking for a job can be challenging, finding the right job can be formidable. The key question is, 'How can we, in this rapidly changing world, make some sensible career decisions?'. In today's increasingly competitive world the era of self-managed careers is upon us. It is our future, no one else's, and the answer to the question, to a large extent, lies in our own hands, and, surprisingly, the Internet.

Although at first glance it may not appear to be much help, estimates indicate there will be 16 million CVs registered on the Internet by 2002, and that currently there are 500,000 jobseekers logging on per month, and 80 per cent of visitors to corporate sites actually visit the careers pages. It all sounds very daunting.

The assessment and selection process, that is not only an integral hurdle we have to pass over in finding the career that best suits us, is a great fund of valuable self-insight. Consider what our prospective employer's intention is; they are trying to achieve the closest fit between the people they appoint and the jobs that have to be done, the right person for the right job. This is not the one-way street it at first appears, for selection is a choice for two parties, us, the individual, and the organisation, and the choice has to be right for both.

Internet recruitment is a relatively new, but fast-evolving concept that is increasing the amount of information available to both parties much earlier in the process than is customary. However, to put it into context it really is a delivery medium: fast, wide-ranging communication via the Internet, facilitating the web-enabled delivery of existing, largely pencil and paper, recruitment and selection processes we may have come across before. In addition to the familiar 'job boards', more and more organisations are developing recruitment pages within their corporate website.

Initially Internet recruitment revolved around the rapid distribution of CVs. While it became very easy to post CVs to multiple sites, this ease really exacerbated an already difficult situation. 'How do we the applicant make our "voice" heard?' 'How do employers deal with an increased number of CVs, ensuring all sifting and shortlisting was accomplished fairly?'

To try and address the issue, the second-generation sites were born, relying on key word-search mechanisms that recognise hard skills or competencies to make sense of the huge number of CVs presented. The third and fourth generations, today's Internet recruitment and selection sites, bring objectivity, including psychometrics, to both processes providing us, the job applicant, with knowledge to help our career management in two key areas.

First, our prospective employer is able to provide much more information than has previously been made available to us through more traditional means, about their organisation, the jobs on offer and, importantly, the organisation's culture and values, issues that are becoming an increasingly important component of the person/job match equation. While on the face of it, a similar job title in two organisations may seem the same, in reality, the jobs can be radically different when organisational culture and values are taken into account, and may well need contrasting attributes for success in the roles. To take advantage of this opportunity an essential start point of our career management is to understand our values, so we are able to map them onto those of the organisation to which we are thinking of applying, in effect creating our own shortlist.

The second opportunity that the Internet brings is for us to gain self-insight. While there are many sites that are purely CV-registration sites, there are a growing number that, having encouraged us to apply, then invite us to complete an application form on-line. (If presented in traditional format we would recognise these as structured and scorable application forms.) Not only do they seek biographical data, they also seek to gain information, via a short question-naire, about our strengths and limitations against competencies (behaviours that lead to success in a role). You may be asked to supply this information either by means of free text boxes or by multiple-choice answers to a short questionnaire, or a combination of both. There will more than likely be facility to print hard copies so that you may, at leisure, give thought to your answers before you reply. The questions will (or should) have been clearly validated and relate to the demands of the job for which we are applying.

The advantage to us is that the information is being gathered, and sifted, about all applicants in the same standardised manner, which in turn will lead to fairer consideration of our application. Clearly, we need to be able to give examples of experiences against various competencies (e.g. leadership, teamwork).

Fourth-generation sites are already emerging, which include on-line psycho-metric assessment. These may be ability tests, personality questionnaires, motivation questionnaires, instruments that are in common use already. Such sites have the facility to incorporate a feedback mechanism that will give us information about our strengths and limitations very early in the selection process. A true source of self-insight to aid self-selection. How should we answer the questions? Just as we would with pencil and paper questionnaires: openly and honestly.

The Internet enables organisations to achieve a much wider marketing reach, that is, exposure to a wider applicant pool. If both parties can reduce the numbers of people that go through the process, we as individuals by focusing only on jobs to which we believe we are well-suited (based on the information we can gain about the jobs and ourselves), and the organisation by only taking forward the most suitable candidates (decisions based on early information gained through Internet recruitment), then there will be less wear and tear on all concerned.

There will be many opportunities throughout our working life for us to push back the frontiers of self-knowledge. The Internet is one. We should fear none, but grasp each one with relish. 'Sometimes it takes two or more people to really know one.' Nowack, 1993

APPENDIX III

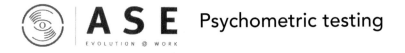 **A S E**   Psychometric testing

Robert A. Edenborough, Managing Consultant, ASE

In applying for a job you are likely to be asked to sit a psychometric test or tests. 'Psychometric' simply means mental measurement and many of the tests are designed to 'measure' mental abilities.

ABILITY TESTS

Ability tests come in a number of forms and the examples shown earlier (see pages 218–225) illustrate some of these. Common types are:

- numerical reasoning
- verbal reasoning
- spatial or mechanical reasoning
- abstract reasoning.

Numerical reasoning tests sometimes pose arithmetical problems of a type familiar from early school days. In other cases, the items require a degree of interpretation and understanding of the type of material being presented as well as calculation. The second type seeks to reproduce some of the situations that people may come across in organisations, such as reading charts of business trends. Usually a high level of mathematical expertise as such is not needed. The demands of doing the test come largely because they have to be completed within a time limit.

Verbal reasoning tests are also of two broad types. Some set tasks like the completion of sentences or the recognition of synonyms. At more advanced levels the format typically involves a passage of prose and a series of statements related to it. The statements have to be judged in terms of whether they reflect information in the passage.

Spatial tests may involve the identification of shapes that may have been rotated or three-dimensional figures to be unfolded. These problems are, however, commonly presented in two-dimensional booklet form. They are used in connection with jobs that require spatial reasoning of some sort which could range from working with engineering design drawings to planning the layout of a store.

Abstract tests are used to assess general reasoning ability. They may be of particular value if candidates are required to deal with entirely new ideas and concepts. They pose problems such as the identification of sequences in abstract patterns.

PERSONALITY

Most personality measures used are of the self-report questionnaire type. Sometimes they ask you to rate how far a particular statement applies to you. In other cases you are asked to choose which of a series of statements is most and which least like you. There is some debate as to whether these should be called tests on the grounds that your personality is what it is and to refer to it in terms of testing is to imply something potentially *wrong* with the essence of who you are. Nevertheless different personalities will fit differently well with different types of job and so in practice when personality measures are used in selection situations there is no doubt that you are being tested. However, the point often made in the introduction to personality questionnaires that there are 'no right or wrong answers' to individual questions is true in the sense that you are not being asked to solve problems but to indicate something about yourself and your typical behaviour.

You may wonder if it is possible to 'cheat' at personality tests. The first response to this must be why would you choose to do so; do you feel that you should be other than you are? If you did 'cheat' and got a job as a result you would be unlikely to be comfortable in the job and probably would not cope. Thus if you thought that some items in a test were to do with orderliness, even though you yourself were rather slapdash in your approach to things and chose all the statements that described you as orderly you would probably not have the systematic approach necessary in the job. You would feel bored, you would probably miss the detail and would be unlikely to last very long. Also it is quite likely that you would not get as far as being offered a job as for many personality measures there are built in checks that give an indication that distortion is occurring.

USE AND INTERPRETATION OF TESTS

An employer will be using ability measures and personality questionnaires to find out broadly how someone will cope with the particular intellectual demands of a job on the one hand and how they will conduct themselves in approaching tasks, interacting with others and perhaps dealing with pressure on the other. In order to make these interpretations your performance will usually be compared with that of a 'norm group' of others. Because of this approach just how difficult an ability test seems to be to you as you go through it may not give you much of a guide as to how you have done, as the interpretation of your performance depends on comparing it with the standard set by the norm group.

Those working with tests and personality questionnaires should abide by professional standards laid down by the British Psychological Society and the Institute of Personnel and Development. Among other things these say that feedback should be given to those tested. If this is not forthcoming when you are tested ask, about it! For personality measures feedback is often used as part of a further discussion with you as the candidate. This is partly to check that the measure is giving a realistic picture of you. It is also to provide further information to expand the indications from the questionnaire. To stick with the example of orderliness, if you appear to be high on this you may be asked to give evidence of situations where you have demonstrated this and where it has been particularly important in the past.

Sometimes ability tests will be used as part of a screening process and sometimes to provide additional information on a group of candidates all of whom have been shortlisted. In the screening case a definite cut-off score is likely to be applied. Where tests and questionnaires are used at the shortlist stage they may often result in a detailed report. This will be considered by a final selection panel along with other information such as that taken from a CV or from a presentation *to* the panel. Professional use of tests also requires that they should never be used as the sole determinant of whether or not someone is offered a job but should be set in the context of such other information.

PREPARING FOR TESTING

The advice for exams of 'get a good night's sleep' applies to testing. It is also a good idea to allow yourself plenty of time to arrive at the testing location and as far as possible to clear your mind of other matters. If you are waiting for the test to finish so that you can dash out and check for messages on your mobile phone you are unlikely to give the test your best shot!

There is also the question of what preparation can be made by practice in advance. The guidance here is to familiarise yourself with the type of material available but not to over-practise which could lead to some distortion. There are a number of effective publications on the market to aid familiarity. Also you will quite often be sent information by an employee to help you prepare for specific tests such as in the illustrations given.

TESTS AND CAREER GUIDANCE

You may, of course, take an initiative in going through tests yourself in order to find out about your capacities and inclinations. A number of bodies offer services of this type. In addition to the ability and personality measures described here you may be asked to take a motivational questionnaire to suggest what your drives and satisfactions are or an interest inventory. These ask you to rate different elements of work and so build up a picture of the type of job that could interest you.

References

Prepare for Tests at Interview: For Graduates and Managers, Robert Williams, Windsor: ASE. Available directly from ASE, Hanover House, 2–4 Sheet Street, Windsor, Berkshire SL4 1BG.

How to Master Selection Tests, M. Bryon and S. Modha, London: Kogan Page.

APPENDIX IV

Leaving the forces?

Mind your language! Now what does he mean by that? All professions have their own jargon and expressions. If you're an accountant looking for a job as an accountant, you can talk to an interviewer in accountantspeak, or a surgeon talking to another surgeon … and so on. If you're 'stepping out' into civvy street you'll need to use a different language from the one you're used to using.

To give you an example. I live in Lincolnshire and there are four RAF bases within 15 minutes' drive. I even get my own private air show occasionally, when the Red Arrows practise over my house! Recently, I was asked to give advice on the CV of a friend of a friend, who is leaving the RAF. The first thing that struck me was his rank/job title which is 'technician'. He's a highly skilled, qualified engineer and is responsible (along with others) for making sure that about 40 million pounds' worth of aircraft works as it should. Years ago I used to be involved in recruiting semi-skilled 'manufacturing technicians', who were process workers on a shampoo production line. Have I made my point? When you write your CV and letters of application, and when you go to interviews, make sure that you explain what your job involves and also your responsibilities, in plain English.

I am extremely grateful for the following contribution from Barbara Walsh, Regional Resettlement Advisor, RAF Brampton:

Many service leavers face difficulties with external job markets because of general lack of visibility of their work within the service. In addition, the smaller numbers of service personnel to meet increasing operational demands mean that opportunities for preparation towards exit are often extremely limited. Service leavers will be moving from a relatively encompassing and paternal organisation, to what is often a hostile environment. Prospective employers may have little or no knowledge of the specialist skills and attributes required to fulfil the service role, or the ways in which these can be mapped across to civilian profes-sions. As a result of this, some employers are hesitant to take on an unknown quantity. In many cases the service leaver will have very narrow experiences of interviews (their last interview may have been when joining up) and this may prevent them from giving a good account of themselves. With this in mind, it is therefore vital to stress the need to use all available time wisely in the compilation of CVs and personal portfolios, and in how to achieve an assured performance at interview.

If you have served in the armed forces, the following may be able to help:

Regular Forces Employment Association, tel 0207 321 2011 for your local branch, or www.rfea.org.uk
Officers' Association, tel 0207 930 0125, or www.oaed.org.uk
SSAFA, tel 0207 403 8783 for your local branch

JOBSEARCH AND CAREER PLANNING WORKSHOPS

Would you like to receive information about jobsearch and career planning workshops based on *3 easy steps to the job you want*?

For further information write to:

Malcolm Hornby c/o Pearson Education

128 Long Acre, London WC2E 9AN

Fax your enquiry to 020 7240 5771

E-mail: enquiries@TheJobSearchersSuperstore.com

Or visit our website www.TheJobsearchersSuperstore.com

FINAL THOUGHTS

The rate of change with modern technology means that some recruiters, like everyone else, will continue to explore new possibilities. I recently mailed a videotape of myself, making a presentation to an imaginary audience, to a company in California. They are using this method to pre-select consultants for a project. A friend of mine from the UK was interviewed by video-cam on the Internet for a job in Australia. The images were jumpy but this was acceptable compared with the cost of flights (she got the job!). I'm told that as more bandwidth becomes available high quality video streaming will become commonplace. Translated into English I understand that this means that (probably by the time this book leaves the printers!) if you've got a video-cam linked to a computer connected to the Internet, recruiters will be able to interview you across the Internet. You'll be able to attend four or five interviews a day without leaving home!

DON'T BE DAUNTED by the new technology if you're camera shy! Remember, all of these new methods used by recruiters are nothing more than tools to help them to make the best decision. They are not an end in themselves. And for the foreseeable future, I believe, interviews in person will continue be our most popular selection method.

Whatever selection methods you encounter, the most important thing to remember is that the recruiter is recruiting a person. Decide what you want out of life. Identify the career and find the job that fits in with your career and life plans. And when you get to the selection process: let the power of your personality persuade them that you are that person!

Once again, good luck.
Malcolm